# JOURNAL FOR THE STUDY OF THE OLD TESTAMENT
## SUPPLEMENT SERIES
# 36

Editors
David J A Clines
Philip R Davies

Department of Biblical Studies
The University of Sheffield
Sheffield S10 2TN
England

# THE SONG
## OF
# FOURTEEN
# SONGS

Michael D. Goulder

Journal for the Study of the Old Testament
Supplement Series 36

Copyright © 1986 JSOT Press

Published by
JSOT Press
Department of Biblical Studies
The University of Sheffield
Sheffield S10 2TN
England

Printed in Great Britain
by Redwood Burn Ltd.,
Trowbridge, Wiltshire.


British Library Cataloguing in Publication Data

Goulder, M.D.
  The Song of fourteen songs.—(Journal for the
  study of the Old Testament supplement series,
  ISSN 0309-0789; 36)
  1. Bible. O.T. Song of Solomon—Commentaries
  I. Title          II. Bible. O.T. Song of Solomon
  III. Series
  223'.9077          BS1485.3

  ISBN 0-905774-86-8
  ISBN 0-905774-87-6 Pbk

# CONTENTS

Preface     vii

Introduction     1

Translation and Commentary
1. The Arrival, 1.1-8     10
2. The Audience, 1.9–2.7     16
3. The Courtship, 2.8-17     22
4. In the Night, 3.1-5     26
5. The Procession, 3.6-11     28
6. The Wedding, 4.1-7     32
7. The Consummation, 4.8–5.1     36
8. A Knock at the Door, 5.2-9     40
9. A Lover Lost and Found, 5.10–6.3     44
10. The One and Only, 6.4-12     48
11. The Dance, 7.1-10     54
12. A Night in the Country, 7.11–8.4     60
13. Love's Demand, 8.5-10     64
14. The Queen, 8.11-14     68

Discussion     71
    The Date     72
    A Doctrine Implied     74
    Love and Sex     79
    A Setting in Israelite Life     80
    Notes     87

Bibliography     91

Index of Biblical and Rabbinic References     93

# PREFACE

The Song of Songs, or Song of Solomon, has been a riddle and a fascination for more than two thousand years, and not least in modern times. It includes some of the most beautiful poetry in the Bible, but it hardly mentions God, if it does at all. The poetry is apparently human love-poetry, even erotic love-poetry. Many theories have been propounded to explain it, some making it an allegory of the divine love, some seeing a ritual background to it, some breaking it into fragments.

I have not been satisfied with any of the current views of the Song, and this little book presents a new view, which is my own. As a new interpretation implies a slightly different understanding of many of the words and phrases in the poem, I have had to make a new translation. The translator has a choice: either he can make a literal translation of the Hebrew, and say in fluent English what he means in the notes, or he can make a fluent version and justify this by reference to the Hebrew in the notes. I have preferred the second; and as the Song is poetry, I have made so bold as to render it into rough English verses—some loose hexameters, and some traditional rhyming lyric meters, as the subject-matter seemed to require. These are set out in the poem's fourteen Songs below, and are intended to form a continuous unity. The reader can read through the whole continuously, and for a general understanding needs to know no more than that there are three speakers, the King, the Princess, and the Chorus.

I hope, however, that many readers will be more curious than this, and I have tried to provide some commentary on the translation, which should be both sufficiently short and readable to be available to them, and also sufficiently detailed and accurate to justify my interpretation to professional scholars. Whether I have succeeded in

this double aim will be for the lay and the learned reader to decide, but I am committed to the belief that scholarly conclusions should be at the disposal of the ordinary educated public; and commentaries of 700 pages cannot be used by the former and are a weariness to the latter. So the reader without Hebrew should not be dismayed by the array of strange italicized words in the Commentary: they are the English form of the original Hebrew words, and the discussion of them is written for him to understand. The brief Introduction, the Commentary on the Translation, and the concluding Discussion, are all intended for him. Only the brief Notes are there for the expert.

To my colleagues in the endeavour to understand the Bible I should stress that, despite my attempt at a broad and general appeal, I am offering a new and serious theory of the Song's origin, purpose and setting in Israelite life. The price of brevity in the Commentary has been the omission of alternative opinions (of which an outline is given in the Introduction, and an apologia for their exclusion); but brevity, they will agree, is a virtue, for which little apology is required. I am grateful to my friend John Eaton, of the Department of Theology in my University, who has kindly read and suggested improvements to the text; to Francis Landy, for a number of valued suggestions; and to Mrs Patricia Costa, Mrs Rachel Crowder, and other enthusiasts, who have helped and encouraged me in the search.

Michael Goulder
September, 1984

# INTRODUCTION

Of the problems raised by the Song of Songs, two are primary, and the remainder wait upon their solution. One of these two is the long-discussed question of the unity of the poem. The Song is often broken down into small sub-units: do these have any sequence, and can they be seen as in any sense a unified whole? The other is the less clearly treated, but often vital dilemma of the author's (or authors') imagination. Does he or do they observe carefully and make precise comparisons for the similes which fill the poem, or is the thinking woolly? It is only when we have made a decision on these two prior problems that we are able to consider a constellation of other questions, such as the Song's setting in Israelite life, its religious message (if any), its gaining a place in the Canon, its interpretation as allegory by the rabbis and Church Fathers, etc. We need first an answer to the two primary questions, and this involves going through the Song, and considering them at each point. So this Introduction, which is to clarify these central problems, is followed by the exposition of the text of the Song, in the Translation and Commentary; only then shall we be in a position to take the Discussion of the secondary problems.

In an article written in 1935, H.H. Rowley divided interpretations of the Song into allegorical (Jewish and Christian), dramatic, liturgical and anthological views:[1] there is a more nuanced analysis in later works, like D. Lys's commentary,[2] but the outline remains. None of these approaches is dead. The allegorical torch has been kept burning by a line of distinguished French Roman Catholic scholars,[3] and by Protestant believers in Biblical inspiration.[4] A sustained drama, with Bride, Bridegroom and Companions, underlies the translation in the New English Bible. The liturgical approach has been recently restated in M.H. Pope's voluminous Anchor Bible Commentary,[5] and is viewed sympathetically by Lys. The anthological approach, in which the Song is taken as a collection of short love-poems, is probably the most widely accepted view, and is represented, for example, by G. Gerleman's Biblischer Kommentar,[6] and R. Gordis's commentary.[7] There are besides recent more literary approaches like that of F. Landy,[8] which could be included in an exhaustive list.

With a work like the Song, a general line of interpretation is either convincing or it is not. The allegorical and liturgical views, even in the modified versions of say A. Robert or Lys, seem to me simply to collapse under the implausibility of their exposition.[9] I do not think that the ideas behind them are valueless, as will appear in the Discussion, but as principles of interpretation they do not succeed. The same has often been true of the dramatic interpretation, whether because of its anachronistic romanticism or because of the complexity of textual alterations, supposed stage directions, and forced exegesis.[10] But the issue between the dramatic and anthological positions is not straightforward. Gerleman and Gordis assume some drama, in the form of at least brief interchanges between the young man, the maiden and a group of some kind, as well as of lyrics spoken by one or the other; so the only distinction is between short, independent dramatic lyrics, and a longer, semi-continuous sequence, in which one scene leads on from another.

Faced with this option, we are in principle bound to choose the sequence if we can, because the hypothesis explains so much more. Of course if the sequence cannot be maintained without considerable emendations, alterations of order, forced exegesis, etc., the hypothesis will collapse from repeated implausibility. But the anthology view is only a counsel of despair: we are driven to it only if proposals of meaningful sequence fail to convince. In the exposition below I have therefore not attempted to rebut allegorists, ritualists, anthologists, or even other dramatists: I have simply expounded the Song as a semi-continuous sequence of fourteen scenes, moving in a progression from the arrival of the Princess at Solomon's court to her acknowledgment by the King as his favourite queen. I have not altered the order of the text at all, nor proposed any emendation to the Hebrew consonants of the Massoretic text (MT); once I have accepted the vowels implied by the Greek Version (LXX) (7.10); and I have supplied half a dozen stage directions where the text seems to imply them. If the reader finds such a progression persuasive, then, I submit, there is no need of further debate.

The following, then, as I understand it, is the 'plot' of the Song. The young woman is an Arabian princess from Nadiv, and in Song 1 she has arrived at Solomon's palace: 'the king has brought me into his chambers'. She expresses passionate love for her royal fiancé, 'let him kiss me . . .', and ends by asking the way to the Audience Chamber, which the Chorus, the ladies of the harem, tell her. Song 2 is in the Audience Hall, where the King greets her with enthusiasm. They embrace ('My beloved is unto me a sachet of myrrh lying between my breasts'), and she begins to speak with a proprietorial tone of the furnishings—'our couch, our house, our rafters'. Thereafter things move quickly. She sits down beside him and kisses him, 'I delight in his shadow and sit down, and his fruit is sweet to my taste'; and the scene ends with his left hand under her head, and his right hand enfolding her. With Song 3 he comes running to court her, and invite her into the country; and she bids him to her bed for the night—not of course to sleep with her, for they are not yet married, but he is to be as a hart on the cloven hills of her breast. In Song 4 she awakes to find the King has gone; she goes after him through the streets and ways of the city, that is the corridors and rooms of the palace. She meets the watchmen, the eunuchs, and the King himself, and takes him back to bed with her. In Song 5 the ladies are watching the Princess in the royal palanquin (*mî zō't*) being carried in procession to her wedding, where the King awaits her on his special new throne (*'appiriōn*) in the crown Bathsheba has given him for the occasion. In Song 6 the King admires her in her wedding veil, praising all the loveliness that he can see, from her eyes and hair down to her breasts. Song 7 is the consummation of their marriage: he bids her to come down from the mountains—that is from her breast—to the garden of her womb, to the sealed spring full of the aromas of desire. She welcomes him into her garden, and he says, 'I have come into my garden, my sister-bride'. It is not until this Song that he calls her his bride, as he now does repeatedly. Song 7 marks the half-way point of the fourteen Songs, and the Consummation is the first of the two high points of the book.

In the second half, from 5.2, the Princess moves from being Solomon's new wife to being his Queen. In Song 8 he knocks on her door, but she is slow in responding, and he goes. She follows but cannot find him, and in Song 9 asks help of the ladies, who are conveniently about in the middle of the night: she describes her love in detail. With Song 10 he returns to her—she cries 'I am my

beloved's and my beloved is mine!' He then tells her that she is his
only love, and has captivated him: even his queens and women salute
her. They make love the second time: 'I went down to the garden of
nuts . . . ' We might think her victory rather easy, so in Song 11 the
ladies call for the return of Abishag the Shunamite: but the Princess
is not having that, and dances for the King herself. This time the
praises move up from her feet, beautiful in their sandals, to her arms
waving like a palm-tree; not much between is omitted, so she is
probably dancing naked. Having now further aroused her husband,
she takes him off to the country in Song 12, where she 'awakens' him
under the apple-tree. In this way she can be hailed in public in Song
13, 'Who is this coming up from the desert?', now her beloved's open
favourite; and she makes the famous and beautiful appeal to him,
'Set me as the seal upon your heart, for love is strong as death, and
jealousy hard as Sheol'. She can only be satisfied to be permanently
with him, and in Song 14 this is put to the test. He is with his nobles
administering his vineyard: she calls to him from the garden, and he
comes.

For the greater part, the fourteen Songs are clearly marked in the
text, usually by the device of a verse to or from the Chorus. What has
obscured this, and the steadily advancing plot which it embodies, is
the second problem with which I began, that of the precision of mind
of the author (if I may, for the moment, refer to him in the singular).
Does he think, observe and express himself precisely, or must we
think of his images as merely 'beautiful', i.e. meaningless, and be
content to regard him as woolly? I will take two instances from ch. 5
to show what I mean.

5.12 runs, 'His eyes are like doves by brooks of water, Bathed in
milk, dwelling by a fullness (*millē't*)'. The force of the images is not
immediately apparent, and some, like Gerleman, opt for the woolly
view: the description refers, he says, to the doves and not the eyes—
indeed he goes so far as to say that this view 'should not be doubted'.
More usually, however, commentators have felt that the phrase
'bathed in milk' is evocative of the white of the eye, and a long line, at
least as far back as Franz Delitzsch,[11] has taken the view that the
poet is thinking of the pupils as like doves, and the milk as the iris.
This is of course an uncomfortable combination of the precise and
the vague: for while the iris is milky in colour, and even texture,
doves are not round or dark like pupils—and furthermore, the Song
several times compares eyes to doves, and only here is the bathing in

milk mentioned. So perhaps we should, if only for the sake of charity, pause a moment and ask if there might not be some other comparison in the author's mind. It is certainly the case that doves, more obviously than other birds, may be observed in pairs, like eyes; but more significantly, the feature that marks out a dove is its fan-like tail. Doves *flutter*; and so do eyes. Could he then be thinking of the eye-*lid* as like the dove's tail? Well, we have a saying, 'Any girl has but to flutter her eyes . . .'; and it is, I believe, common experience that movement of the eye-lashes is attractive to the opposite sex. What is more, this thought appears to have been familiar to the Hebrews, for their word for an eye-lid is 'ap'ap, from 'ûp to fly—a 'fly-fly'. So we could, boldly but charitably, suppose that the poet is a close observer, both of nature and of lovers. The doves (tails) are the eye-lids, the milk is the iris, and the bathing is the movement which one can see as a bird splashes water over itself with its tail. Then the 'fullness' will be the pupil. Tur-Sinai cites Gen. R. 95 as a passage where *millē't* means a pool (see n. 38), and the pupil does indeed look like a full pool with its dark depths: and the Song makes the same comparison later, 'Your eyes are pools in Heshbon'. 'Beside brooks of water' could easily be a reference to the tear-ducts which keep the eyes moist.

In this way it has been possible to give some account of each of the details of the language; but the reader must be in two minds. It makes the poem more interesting; but is it right? There is no means of deciding on the basis of one verse. If this is right, it involves a general theory about the whole poem. If I am asserting a precise meaning for 5.12, I am asserting a precise imagination for the author, and that means for every verse in the Song. The Translation and Commentary are the examination of that assertion. Nonetheless, the hypothesis that the poet thinks precisely is so crucial that I offer a second and more difficult instance now, from the same chapter.

Having spoken of her beloved's eyes, the princess moves down his body. We can all see that his head, hands and feet being of gold might well have reference to the pleasant golden colour of the exposed part of his person; or 'his legs are pillars of alabaster' probably likens them to the veining in marble columns. But what are we to make of 5.14b, 'His *mē'îm* are an 'ešet of ivory, inlaid with lapis lazuli'—or possibly 'sapphires'? Our first problem is not knowing what is meant by *mē'îm*. The word normally means the inward parts, but clearly here it is a description of something we can see, and most commentators take it to mean the belly. The movement is down the body, and we are moving from the hands in v. 14a to the legs in v. 15a, so the belly would be quite suitable. As the *'ešet* is a hapax (that is, it occurs only this once in the Bible), one can translate hopefully, 'his belly is a plaque of ivory'—something nice and flat. Lys then adds even more hopefully that this is confirmed by the 'incrustations' following, which 'make one think of the blue veins on the surface of the skin': but the fact is, surely, that there are no blue veins visible in this part of the anatomy. Late Jewish comments, however, suggest that an *'ešet* of ivory is long and thin, and Jastrow's dictionary gives the translation 'column'. Cant. R. 5.14 says that one can 'make many pegs and darts' from it, and Yalkut Cant. 991 says that the scrolls of the law are like it. So Gordis, and Delitzsch before him, took *mē'îm* to be the trunk of the body; though here too it must be said that veining is hardly to be noticed on the human torso, whereas it is prominent in the limbs. So I ask myself, is there a part of the male body, between the hands and the legs, which is heavily veined, and which at all resembles a column of ivory? Indeed, comes the answer, there is; and furthermore, what is a column of ivory but a tusk? And to an enthusiastic bride, such as we have portrayed in the Song, a tusk of ivory might seem a very potent image. *mē'îm*, then, will be used in a slightly euphemistic sense, as when the promise is made to Abraham, 'He that shall come out of thy own *mē'îm* shall be thy heir'. We use the word 'loins' in the same euphemistic way in English.

It will be seen that this issue over precision is the same as the issue over sequence. Two swallows do not make a summer, and it might be that we cannot extend the precision hypothesis to other texts in the poem without becoming grossly implausible. So the normal, (rather) woolly view could be right still; but it is a counsel of despair, like the anthology view. If we *can* make believable sense of the poem on the hypothesis of the author's accuracy, then we should, just as we should try out the hypothesis of a sustained sequence of plot. In what follows I am simply carrying through these two basic possibilities without constantly noting the woolly or anthological alternatives. My only (and sufficient) task is to carry the reader with me in the conviction that the overall view of the poem that results is believable.

My response to the two basic questions with which I began carries a number of corollaries. The first and most acceptable of these is that we are dealing with a single author. For a single structure or plot to the poem can only come from the activity of a single mind, never mind how much tradition he is working with; and if we find the same precision of thought and observation everywhere, that will be a confirmation of this conclusion. Hence I shall speak of 'the author/ poet' in the singular now without further apology.

The second corollary may not find such easy acceptance. It is that at least the surface meaning of the Song is straightforwardly erotic. There may be other levels of meaning, and to these I shall return in the Discussion; but it will be sufficiently clear from what I have written already that the plot I have described makes sense only as a love-story, and that of an erotic rather than a romantic kind. The poet follows his couple through every intimacy, with a stream of charming double-entendres, euphemisms and delicate indirectnesses— the cloven hills, the garden of nuts, 'I have come into my garden'. The rather frequent allusion to breasts is, and is intended to be, arousing; and the same goes for 'his loins' and other matters on which I have yet to touch. Now it is the nature of double-entendre that the unfamiliar reader will find himself surprised, and perhaps shocked, that what at first seemed an innocent and beautiful scene can be thought to carry a second, erotic meaning. I take an illustration from 8.5.

'Under the apple-tree I awakened you; there your mother writhed with you, there she who bore you writhed.' At first sight we have an idyllic moment. The young couple have been out under the stars for the night, and chose the famous apple-tree where David slept with Bathsheba, and Solomon himself was conceived. She was awake first in the dawn light, and roused her husband from his dreams. But, even without my general interpretation, doubt begins to stir. Why is it thought necessary to give such a physical description of the conception (if, as is usually thought, this is the meaning)? Why is it mentioned twice? Why the emphatic double 'there'? And surely, even if things were rough in David's time, he will have slept with his wives, and even his mistresses, comfortably in bed in the privacy of the palace? So the suspicion is evoked that 'I awakened you' (with 'you' masculine in the Hebrew text) refers to sexual arousal, and that is the half-way house taken by Gordis, Lys and others, with some speculation on the aphrodisiac powers of the apple. But if, as I am supposing, the author is not partly vague (or obscure), but of a single and clear cast of mind, the possibility must occur to us that 'Under the apple-tree' is also a phrase with a double meaning. For it could be that the place where she aroused him is an anatomical place as well as a place in a glade; and that it is thought of as an apple-tree by virtue of the two fruits hanging down above the 'trunk'; that there is a special force to 'under', because it is at the under end of this tree that the nerves are concentrated that make for such arousal; and it is 'there' that women (including Bathsheba) are in turn aroused to ecstasy in the moment of union. Of course the apple-tree is a common feature of the Song, and if this suggestion is to be taken seriously it will reflect on other passages: but, as we shall see, it seems to shed light on them too.

I have chosen this illustration because, although it is as delicate and allusive as usual, it is not quite so charming; and the Song can sail nearer the wind than this. But to far the greater number of those who have read the Song with attention, such a suggestion must seem grossly offensive. They have seen the Song as a revelation of God's love to Israel, or of his mystical being, or of Christ's love of the soul, or of the paradoxes of Paradise (to use Francis Landy's title); and the suggestion of a primarily sexual meaning on a detailed level is bound to seem, at the least, a great disappointment. Many of those who have loved the Song most have been ascetics and religious—we are walking in the steps of Aqiba, Origen and St John of the Cross. So it is not surprising that when J. Cheryl Exum makes a series of sexual interpretations, John Healey objects that they are unnecessary.[12] André Robert regards such approaches as unspiritual and 'licencieux',[13] and I have been criticized myself by a Professor of English as being pedestrian and unsubtle.

Professors of literature may concern themselves with the meaning of a text apart from the intention of its author; but my concern is a historical one. I am trying to find out the meaning of the Song as its author intended it. For the purpose, surely, it is not a valid criticism of Exum to say that her suggestions are unnecessary. It may properly be said that she only attempts to make sense of parts of the Song, cut up on a scheme of literary parallels that is not very convincing, and that this leads her into sometimes overdoing the sexual euphemism; but her suggestions are sometimes illuminating. If they seem to be right, then that is what we are after. Similarly with Robert and other critics. It will be disappointing if the author turns out to be a licentious or pedestrian man. But our task is to find out if he was, and if the two principles of interpretation I have adopted above turn out to be satisfying, we should be able to say. I hasten to reassure the reader that I think the answer is no.

There is, however, a limitation the other way, which my principles impose, and which may meet a similar resistance. Poetry is often valued for the richness of its ambiguities, enabling the reader to find a multiplicity of meaning; and erotic poetry, with its built-in use of double entendre, may take an especial delight in such ambiguity. Thus in 5.2ff. the voice of the King is heard saying, 'Open', and two verses later, 'My beloved put forth his hand (*yādô*) from the hole'. This has seemed to many to whom the erotic interpretation is natural a straightforward set of euphemisms; the king speaks as if he is knocking on a door, but it is another kind of door he wishes the princess to open, and the hole is not really that through which the latch passes; and even 'hand' is sometimes used euphemistically in the Bible (Isa. 56.5). But if we take these expressions so, we shall find it hard to make sense of the intervening lines; and, as will be seen in the comments on the passage, I think that all that is intended here is a real door and latch, and a hand with five fingers. Of course, the euphemistic meaning may have occurred to the author also, and he may have put it in as a kind of tease; for he means to titillate, and double-entendre is a technique for titillation, even when the surface meaning is all that applies.

One last initial hesitation should be stilled. It is sometimes objected against the nineteenth-century drama theories that there is no instance of a drama in the Bible; and the same absence of precedent may be felt to tell against my own proposal. The difficulty does not seem serious, however, for the Song is unique in the Bible, and any theory—allegory, liturgy, anthology included—will find it hard to provide adequate Biblical precedent. Moreover, the Book of Job is not far removed, being a continuous sequence of answering speeches in poetry; the main difference is that the poetry is set in a prose framework (Job 1–2, 42), and is punctuated by 'stage directions' such as, 'Then Job answered and said'. Furthermore, two of the oldest manuscripts of the Song that we have, the Greek codices Sinaiticus and Alexandrinus of AD 350-400, set the text out with stage directions: 'the groom to the bride', 'the bride to the guards', etc. So not only is there something similar to a drama in Job as well as the Song, but this was the way in which our early manuscript tradition understood it.

# Song 1

*The Arrival*

1.1 Solomon's Song of Songs.
   2    *Princess*
        With his mouth let him kiss me with kisses.
        For better than wine is your loving, (3) and rich of scent are your
            ointments.
        Even your name is ointment of gold—that is why the girls love you.
   4  Summon me after you; we will come running: for now that the king
            has
        Brought me into his halls, you shall be our joy and our gladness.
        More than of wine will we tell of your loving, for more than the
            handsome
        You do they love. (5) I am dark but lovely, O daughters of Zion,
        Dark as the tents of Kedar, dark as Solomon's curtains.
   6  Stare at me not though darkened I be, that the sun has beheld me;
        Hot with me too were my mother's sons, and made me a worker
        Out in the vineyards at home—my vineyard, my own, have I worked
            not.
   7  Tell me, you whom my soul is in love with, where do you pasture?
        Where do you make to lie down in the noon?
        Lest I become like a woman in veils by the flocks of your comrades.
   8  *Chorus*
        Follow the track if you know not the way, O fairest of women,
        That the flocks have trodden, and feed your kids by the tents of the
            shepherds.

[1.1]   Usually taken to mean 'the supreme song', as 'the holy of holies' means 'the holiest place'. But Song is not a word of value like 'holy'; a closer parallel is 'the heaven of heavens' (1 Kgs 8.27), i.e. comprising the lesser heavens, or our 'the book of books', i.e. the book comprising the lesser books. The Song comprises fourteen lesser, clearly demarcated Songs. The *'ªšer* ('which [is] of S.'), instead of the regular *še-*, shows that 1.1 is not original to the Song, and the verse is the earliest commentary on it: the 'youth' was taken to be Solomon from very early. The frequency of the name, of 'king', and of royal appurtenances (ointments, litter, escorts of soldiers, etc.), make this the natural understanding, and it seems to me to be right.   [2]   The speaker's enormous confidence shows that she has no plebeian standing: she constantly takes the initiative, even with the king, and her tone towards the 'daughters of Jerusalem' is throughout superior, verging on arrogance, while theirs to her is compliant to submissive. Verse 4, with its easy switches from first person singular to plural and back, shows that she has come with an escort of maidens; and the final phrases show that they are also to be part of the seraglio. 7.2 calls her 'daughter of *nādîb*' (on which see below). It seems that we shall not be misled if we think of her as a princess. She is arriving at Solomon's court (v. 4b), and would be welcomed by the king with a kiss (cf. Gen. 29.22), but formally, cheek to cheek. But she is in love with him, and wants to be kissed mouth to mouth. She expects the kissing to be intimate, and his taste to be better than wine (2.4; 4.10; 7.10).

[3]   Verses 2b-3a are a chiasmus: 'For good are your lovings beyond wine; as to scent your ointments are good'. The chambers are made fragrant with scented oils, and this leads to the thought of the anointed king himself, whose name, Solomon, is derived from *šlm*, fullness, richness. The play between *šēm*, name, and *šemen*, oil, recurs in Eccl. 7.1, and is feebly rendered by the assonance name/ointment. *tûraq*, which Gerleman plausibly conjectures as a noun from *yrq*, green yellow (cf. *šemen ra'ªnān*, Ps. 92.11), should indicate the richness of the oils, which will be fresh green in the autumn (Ps. 92), but golden-green in maturity (Ps. 68.14, *yᵉraqraq*). The rich scents stir the princess and her maidens alike to feelings of desire for the king.

[4]   *moškēnî*, draw, conduct me 'after you'; i.e. send a eunuch so that I can take my place in your procession into the throne-room. *mšk* is used of 'drawing' in love at Hos. 11.4. The company's

enthusiasm is shown by their willingness to run instead of guarding their dignity; and only the princess is to be sent for, but the whole party means to respond (cohort.). Her recent arrival is testified in v. 4b, 'the king has brought me into his chambers', i.e. the inner rooms reserved for the womenfolk. The joy and gladness echo Ps. 45.15, where the foreign bride and her virgin companions are similarly brought to the king. *mēyᵉšārîm* should be a comparison introduced by *m(in)*, than, in v. 4c, parallel to *miyyayin*, 'than wine'; and this sense is given if *yāšār* is understood as 'well-built', rather than just 'upright', as in 2 Kgs 10.3. The girls, like their mistress, have fallen for the king, rather than any good-looking young man they might fancy. In this way we get a second chiasmus, as in vv. 2b-3a, 'We shall speak of your loves more than wine, more than handsome men they love you'. The bridesmaids will be among the 'virgins' (6.8) of the seraglio, and in course of time will be able to compare notes with their mistress on the king's prowess as a lover.

[5]     The princess is said to be 'black' (*šᵉḥôrâ*), a characteristic not admired (v. 6a), and contrasting with the king's 'ruddy' complexion (5.10). The word normally means 'black', but need not imply that she is a negress: dark women were called 'black Jane', etc., in eighteenth-century England.[14] The 'daughters of Jerusalem' (Zion) are the other women in the king's harem. Verse 5b implies what is confirmed in 6.12ff., that the princess's home is in northern Arabia. The two similes refer, the one to the home she has come from, the other to the home she is coming to. Tents and curtains are a regular pair in the OT. Here the tents of Kedar, woven of black goats' hair, and the curtains Solomon made for the Temple (2 Chron. 3.14), dyed dark with blue and purple and crimson, are alike symbols of the princess's extremely dark skin; and this requires some explanation, since the poet goes to every length elsewhere to stress her beauty. Of course v. 6 excuses the fact: but why, we have to ask, if Israelite gentlemen preferred blondes, is she not a blonde? She is said to be black as the tents of Kedar, and we should not minimize this by thinking of her as bronzed, as Lys does. It could be that the poet has the Queen of Sheba in mind. Pliny writes of Saba as in Southern Arabia,[15] but Gen. 25.2 and Job 1.15 clearly envisage it as in northern Arabia.[16]

[6]     'Do not look at me that I am a darkie, that the sun has seen me': the poet connects *šᵉḥarḥōret* (root *šḥr*) with *niḥᵃrû* (root *ḥrh*)— as she was darkened by the sun, so were her brothers incensed, angry with her. Given the ancient (and modern[17]) subjection of Arab

women, it is no surprise that a princess should be treated like this:
indeed, harsh treatment of younger royal hero(in)es is the stuff of
folklore. Laban had some authority over his sister Rebecca in Gen.
24, even in her father's lifetime. The princess's father is never
mentioned, and must be presumed dead: her 'mother's sons' are not
true brothers to her, but maltreat her, like the wicked stepmothers of
our tradition. The vineyards are introduced deliberately to lead up to
the reference to her 'own' vineyard, the first of many sexual double-
entendres. Ancient vineyards (again, like modern ones) had the vines
planted in rows, with a limited space between so as to save land.[18]
They were trained over trees, and in summer the vines put forth a
luxuriant growth of tendrils, leaving a narrow passage between the
rows. They thus make an obvious sexual symbol for a woman: note
the emphasis, 'my vineyard that is mine'. The princess has not 'kept'
(*nṭr*), viz. worked, her own vineyard, i.e. she has retained her
virginity.

[7]    Israelite kings were shepherds to their people, and shepherds
pasture their flocks, and make them rest in the midday sun. Solomon
'pastures' too, but it is not sheep that he makes to lie down. Charles
Doughty testifies to sexual relaxation 'in the noon' among the North
Arabian Bedouin.[19] The object is omitted in both v. 7a and v. 7b (cf.
Isa. 13.20 and Gen. 37.16, 'Tell me, where are they shepherding [sc.
the flock]?'). Pasturing is a common sexual image in the Song: the
shepherd directing his sheep to the grass around a spring provided a
ready suggestion of a similar activity between man and woman. The
princess first thinks of herself as a ewe lying down in the noon; she
would like to know where, as she does not want to find herself left
out. If that happened, she might never be accepted into the king's
household, and could end up 'with the flock of your companions', i.e.
as the wife of one of the nobles, also mentioned in 8.13. That would
be heart-breaking, since it is the king she is in love with, and she
would be *kᵉʿōṭyâ*, like a woman covered in veils, that is in mourning.
Israelite women wore mourning when they were widowed, as British
women did till recently (Gen. 38.14; 2 Sam. 14.2): she would not of
course wear widow's weeds at her wedding to such a third party, but
she would feel like it (*kᵉ*).

[8]    is spoken by the 'daughters of Jerusalem', who act as a chorus
throughout the Song, and often, as here, bridge the gap between one
scene and the next. The imagery is developed from v. 7: the corridor
from the women's quarters to the king's apartments becomes the

track that the flocks have trodden. The king and his courtiers there
are the shepherds in their tents. The princess, thought of by virtue of
her position as a shepherdess, is encouraged to take her 'kids', her
bridesmaids, along with her, and try their luck. It is the subtlety of
the double-entendre which constitutes the delightfulness of the Song
throughout.

# Song 2

*The Audience*

*King*
1.9  I would compare you, my friend, to my mare in the chariots of
       Pharaoh:
 10  Fair are your cheeks with the rings in your ears, and your neck with
       pearlstrings.
 11  Ear-rings of gold shall we make you, a necklace with links of silver.
*Princess*
 12  As the king lay on his couch, my spikenard sent forth its fragrance.
 13  A sachet of myrrh is my loved one to me, that lies in my bosom;
 14  A cluster of henna my love is to me, in the vines of En-Gedi.
*King*
 15  Fair is my friend, how fair! And your eye-lids flutter like doves.
*Princess*
 16  Fair is my loved one, and handsome; our bed too is fresh from the
       greenwood.
 17  The beams of our house are cedars, the rafters are cypress.
2.1  I am a rose of the plain, a lily deep down in the valleys.
*King*
  2  Like to a lily that blooms among thorns is my friend among women.
*Princess*
  3  Like an apple by trees in the wood, so is my love among men:
     I delight in its shade, and sit down, and its fruit is sweet to my palate.
  4  Into the chamber of wine he brought me; his standard is on me,
  5  Love—O sustain me with raisins, with apples support me;
     I am in fever with love!
  6  His left hand is under my head, and his right hand enfolds me.
  7  I put you on oath, by the roes and the hinds, you daughters of Zion,
     Stir not love in your king, nor awaken it till it shall please him.

[1.9-11]    The change of scene is evident from the king's presence: we have moved from the Ladies' Common Room to the Audience Chamber, with the king reclining on the royal couch (v. 12). He welcomes the princess with surprised compliments: the marriage has been arranged without meeting, and she might have looked like Anne of Cleves. Lit. 'I have likened you to my mare . . . ' is misleading. Girls would have been no more flattered then than now to be told that they looked like horses. The comparison is between her ear-rings and necklaces and the brass bit and shining caparison of the royal mare. Egyptian love-lyrics cited by Gerleman which compare girls to horses are concerned with their fleetness of foot; and Lys's suggestion that women were valued for their broad haunches for child-bearing is really too unromantic. Horses and chariots alike were imported by Solomon from Egypt (1 Kgs 10.28f.); hence 'the chariots of Pharaoh'. The poet will return to the image in another sense at 6.12. The king calls the princess *ra'ātî*, 'my companion', used throughout the Song as a term of endearment. She will not be his bride till after the wedding, but the word is an encouragement: this does not have to be merely a political marriage.

[10]    The 'turns' (*tōrîm*) on the princess's cheeks must be ear-rings, in parallel with her necklace, rather than plaits or curls: it is good manners for a lover to speak appreciatively of his girl's adornment first, and to come to more personal matters later. NH *ḥᵃraz* is used of stringing pearls and jewels, and it is these that are intended, not beads or shells—she is not a working girl.    [11] Nonetheless the king, with his boundless wealth, can make her look more striking still, in gold and silver. *nᵉquddôt*, 'points' of silver, must be intended to supersede the pearls/stones that now surround her neck, and will be the silver medallions comprising the necklace (cf. 4.4).

[12-14]    Verse 12 is spoken by the princess aside, and makes the situation plain. The king is reclining on his couch (cf. Jastrow on b. Sabb. 63a) as she enters. She is perfumed with nard, an expensive Indian (aphrodisiac) ointment: but 'my nard', as at 4.14, is likely to imply more personal scents (cf. 'my vineyard')—she feels herself to be flowing with passion as she goes forward to greet the king.

[13]    Women wore leather sachets of powdered myrrh 'between the breasts' (m. Sabb. 6.3), and the wording implies a move. He has risen to greet her, and they are standing and embracing. As she hugs him to herself, he is like a bag of perfume between her breasts.

[14]   Henna flowers in June:[20] the strongly scented blossoms are creamy coloured, and are borne in long clusters, not unlike English Buddleia flowers (photo, Zohary, 190). The vineyards of En-gedi were probably famous, or their mention would not be pointed, but there is a sexual symbolism to the name. *'En* means a spring (cf. 4.12, 15), and *gᵉdî* a kid. The princess's bridesmaids have already been spoken of as 'kids' (v. 8), and there has been play with the vineyard symbol in v. 6. So while at one level he is a sachet between her breasts, at another he is a spike (*'eškōl*) of henna flowers in the vines of the Spring of the Kid. Her nard has sent forth its fragrance to good effect.

[15-17]   The king now admires her natural good looks. Lit. 'your eyes are doves': the similitude arises from doves' consorting in pairs, and from the dove's spread tail-feathers, which flutter like eyes (see Introduction).   [16]   The lady returns the compliments; which extend to the furniture ('too'). Her status is considerable, as is implied by the proprietorial 'our bed', 'our house', 'our beams': she is no mere concubine. A royal bed would be kept fresh by being strewn daily with new-cut foliage or rushes, especially in the period of fresh growth from April to June. She appreciates this, and in her imagination turns the hall into an arbour. The sawn, planed beams are seen as if they were still growing trees—cedars, with which Solomon famously panelled his palace (1 Kgs 7.2ff.), and cypresses (1 Kgs 6.34; etc.) for the roofbeams. Lys thinks the precise equivalents are pines and junipers, but we need the traditional names for the Solomonic echoes. If the scene were a real arbour, as is sometimes thought, roofbeams would be difficult to arrange from vertically growing cypresses or junipers. 'Our house' is in the plural in Hebrew, as befits a palace.

[2.1-3]   In so splendid a glade, says the princess playfully, she is nothing but a plain wild flower. Which wild flower we do not know: the 'rose of the plain' is not the Rose of Sharon, but may be the crocus, or the Lilium Colchicum (I. Löw[21]). M. Zohary,[22] p. 176, identifies it with the (Madonna) lily, Lilium Candidum, which also grows wild in Palestine, and this may be right. But the lily (which is also specified) is not a symbol of virgin purity in the Song. It is singled out not only for its beauty and its scent, but also its deep calyx: 'a lily of the valleys' is a further example of a simile which can be taken quite innocently, but which is also sufficiently suggestive in phrasing to ensure that a second intention is present. To be aware of these recurrent double-entendres is, on one level, to understand the

Song.    [2]    The king accepts the lily image, and dignifies it—also a
common technique in the Song, cf. 1.7f.    [3]    But if she excels
among the plants below, how much more does he among the trees
above! *tappûaḥ* is something of a problem. Traditionally it is the
apple-tree, and I have retained this translation. It is a fruit-tree, along
with vine, fig, pomegranate and palm, in Joel 1.12; in the Song its
fruit is support to the love-sick (2.5) and is sweet to the taste (2.3) and
in scent (7.8). Lys cites P. Fournier's opinion that apples had not
been imported in biblical times; he suggested the lemon, but lemons
are not very sweet. NEB suggests the apricot, and a medlar has also
been proposed; but Zohary, p. 70, accepts the traditional apple. As
with the henna and the vines, the apple forms a suggestive pair to the
lily, with its fruit often borne in pairs along a rising spur.    [3b]    The
verbs 'delight' and 'sit down' should not be taken together ('*to* sit')
despite common opinion. Stage directions have not been invented,
and the poet makes use of his text to imply the action. At 1.12 the
king was reclining on his couch, and the princess standing; at 1.13f.
he has risen and is embracing her; at 2.3 she sits down on 'their bed',
and by 2.6 his left hand is under her recumbent head, and his right
hand enfolding her. As was implied in 1.2, she is of a passionate
nature, and is not hesitant about encouraging her fiancé. The
sweetness of the fruit to her palate suggests that they now kiss, and
this is confirmed in what follows.

[4-6]    In 1.2 kisses were compared to wine. The king now 'has
brought me into the wine-house', that is, he welcomes her tongue to
kiss his (cf. 5.16; 7.10). This action releases feelings of passion in
them both, and she lies down beside him (v. 6). She can tell the
strength of his feelings by 'his standard' on her. The ancients did not
have flags as we do, but standards, that is poles held upright with a
symbol on them, SPQR for the Romans, very likely the star of David
for the Israelites. Gerleman is probably right in suggesting that
public houses may have had such standards, as in ancient Arabia: it
would be uncharacteristic of the Song to move from a drinking to a
military metaphor so quickly. The realization that he is responsive
tells her triumphantly that he feels for her genuinely—lit. 'his
standard upon me is love'. It is a limitation which we shall notice
again in the poem that no proper distinction is drawn between
physical and emotional response (cf. 8.8). Her head swims in ecstasy
and she calls to her girls to assist her. But once more we have a
double-entendre. Of the verbs, *smk* can mean both to support

literally (Jg. 16.29) and to sustain as with food (Gen. 27.37); *rpd* can mean the first (cf. 3.10, the back of the throne)—we may assume it also means the second, though we have no evidence. So the words can be an appeal for food—raisin-cakes and apples. But the *'ašîšôt* are also mentioned in Hos. 3.1 in a context which implies that raisin-cakes were offered in pagan worship with sexual overtones ('paramour ... adulteress'). So we should reckon with the possibility that the *'ašîšâ* was baked in the shape of a French loaf rather than an Eccles cake; and that it and the 'apples' could be thought to support her in another sense.     [6]   could be a wish also, as the verb I have translated 'enfolds' could be either that or a present; but we should then expect some such verb with the left hand. A present would make a contrast with the completed 'he brought me' in v. 4.

[7]   Passionate kissing is all very well, but they are not yet married, so the scene must fade on its climax. The princess must go now, but she does not want her lover distracted, so she warns the women of the harem not to excite him by dancing round with nothing on (cf. 7.2ff.), not to stir him to love 'till it (fem., i.e. love) delight' (sc. 'him'). His natural desire, she reckons, will be for her. The roes and the hinds of the field, by whom she adjures them, are a play on words: *ṣebā'ôt* means the hosts of heaven as well as roes, and *'ayelôt haśśādeh*, the hinds of the field, has consonants close to *'ēl šaddai*, God Almighty. They are feminine non-expletives, like 'My sainted aunt'.

# Song 3

*The Courtship*

*Princess*

2.8    My love! He comes! I hear his call!
        He leaps the hills, he skips the height.
9        As hart or fawn my love is light—
    'Tis he, he's stopping by our wall.
    Across the latticed sill he spies,
10       My love, and bids me,

*King*

                        'Come, my friend,
11       The rain is spent and at an end,
    The winter's past—my fair one, rise!
12    Flowers deck the earth, birdsong the air;
       The turtledove coos in our land;
13       The green figs' ripening is at hand;
    The vines their scented blossoms bear.
    Rise! Come, my fair! My dove, take flight!
14       In clefts of rock and covert sheer,
       Your sight I'll see, your voice I'll hear—
    For sweet your voice, and fair your sight.
15    Then take us there the fox-cubs tender,
       The foxes that despoil the vine:
    Our vines their blossoms' perfumes render.'

*Princess*

16       Oh! I am my love's, and he is mine,
    Who feeds in lily-banks! Till dawn
17       Its breezes blow, and shadows flee,
       Come back, be a gazelle, love, be
    Upon the cloven hills a fawn!

To be an addition to a harem the size of Solomon's does not mean that one can automatically expect any attention: the sequence expresses the princess's delight that the king is actually courting her.

[8] His keenness is shown by his running, and calling from a distance: lit. 'The voice of my beloved! Lo, he comes!' He is thought of as running across the undulating palace garden—like the seraglio garden at Topkapi. [9] The imagery is suggested (as often) by the preceding. The Ladies were adjured 'by the hinds ($\check{s}^e b\bar{a}'\hat{o}t$) and the roes ($'ay^el\hat{o}t$) of the field'; now the king is (running) like a hart or gazelle ($\check{s}^eb\hat{\imath}$), or the young of the deer ($'ayy\bar{a}l\hat{\imath}m$). 'Our wall' is the wall of the apartments occupied by the princess and her retinue; it could not be the wall of the maiden's parents' house, as is often proposed—lovers behaving like the king would have angry fathers and brothers after them. '$\hat{o}m\bar{e}d$, 'he is stopping', lit. 'standing', cf. 1 Sam. 9.27; 2 Sam. 2.28. [9c] Lit. 'he gazes from the window, he peeps from the lattice'.

[10f.] All the invitation is at the beginning in Heb., and I have transposed the winter and the rain. The 'latter rains' are finished early in May:[23] the Israelite year falls into two halves, the wet winter and the dry summer.

[12] Lit. 'The flowers are seen on the earth, the time of the singing has come'. Palestine is rich in species of flowers, whose blooming spans the year, but the peak is in April, with slightly smaller numbers in March and May. Elsewhere in the Bible (8x) *zamîr* means a song, but the existence of the verb *zmr* II, to prune, has suggested the translation 'pruning', a second vine-pruning in the spring being a possible reference. But when *all* the other elements are from nature, and none from man's activities, this seems unlikely. Birdsong leads on naturally too to the cooing of the turtledove, a summer migrant. 'Our land', which would not be a natural expression for two co-nationals, is suited to the king welcoming a foreign princess to the beauties of the land of Israel. [13] Lit. 'the fig has reddened the green fruit' (though *ḥnṭ* elsewhere means 'embalm'). The *paggîm* are the small green figs, which in some varieties are carried over the winter and turn red in May and June.[24] 'And the vines (are all) blossom, they give scent': Dalman writes, 'The (vine-) flowers start in May—I saw them near Jerusalem at their beginning on 10th May, 1909. The middle of June was regarded as their peak in *bir zet*. The yellowish-green, strongly-smelling blossoms form a cluster.'[25]

In the second half of the courtship-song, the imagery of the first half is taken up and made more evidently sexual; for the passage is less innocent, though not less beautiful, than is supposed by unwary headmistresses reading it out in school assemblies. Nor is any of it the sheer unparalleled delight in nature for itself which surprises more sophisticated commentators. We have seen that vines are sexually symbolic of women; and figs, like apples, are of men, with their pendant clusters of fruits.

[14] The singing birds and the cooing turtle-dove now suggest the thought that the princess herself, not just her eyes, may be dove-like: 'Rise, come, my friend; my fair one, come; my dove . . . ' As wild doves fly off to mate in remote rocks,[26] so is she to do the same with her royal lover. The clefts, and perhaps also 'the hidden place of the steep ascent', are sexual symbols like the lily and the valleys in 2.1. He says, 'Make me see your sight (*mar'êk*)', which, despite the parallel with 'voice', does not mean her face, which he can see now, and could from her entry in 1.9: he wants to see all of her. (Lys has no justification for thinking that she is hiding behind the lattice: the king can see that she is beautiful, and says so).

[15] 'Take hold (2nd pl. impv.) for us of foxes, little foxes' follows on from 'Make me see/hear . . . ' (2nd sg. impv.). Fox-cubs, with their long, slim muzzles ending in rounded tips, make ideal male sex-symbols, suggested by the perfume-laden vines which are female sex-symbols, and which they do in fact despoil in later summer.[27] When she has shown him her form and spoken lovingly to him (v. 14c), they will be united together. $m^e\d{h}abb^e l\^im$, despoiling, may be a further double entendre, as the word means 'conceiving' at 8.5 (bis); there are similar double meanings for *'ah$^a$bâ*, leather/love, and perhaps *mēy$^{(e)}$šārîm*, than handsome men/uprightness (euph.), elsewhere in the poem. But the action of the fox-cub's muzzle, poking up into the vines, may be sufficiently suggestive. Foxes damage the crop by taking the grapes, not the blossom, so we should translate the $w^e$ lit., '*But* our vines are (in) blossom'.

[16] The king's courting, and invitation, and evident attraction to her, draw from the princess an ecstatic response: he is hers, and she his, 'he who pastures in the lilies'. He called her a lily among thorns at 2.2, and here also lily stands for a beautiful woman. 'Pastures', in Heb. as in English, may be transitive (as at 1.7), or intransitive, as here: he has the run of a whole harem of attractive girls, and he cares for her!     [17]     She is not actually thinking of his romantic expedi-

tion (and perhaps he was not either), but of welcoming him to her bed for the night: not 'let us go', but '(re-)turn (sc. to me)'. 'Till the day blows' shows that he is invited for the night: the breeze rises at both dusk and dawn in Palestine, and *nešep*, blowing time, is used of morning (Ps. 119.147; Job 7.4) as well as evening (Gordis). 'Till the shadows flee' most naturally has the same sense. The song ends as it began, with the king as a deer or young gazelle. Then he leaped the hills as he ran; now he is bidden to the cloven hills of her breast. *bāter* is sometimes taken to mean the spice malobathrum, in line with references to the princess's perfumed breasts in 4.5f. and 8.14; but the Hebrew root always elsewhere means 'cleave', and what could be more suitable? The limitation of invitation to her breasts is intentional, for they are not yet married: 'petting', yes, 'heavy petting', no.

Is the author drawing here on a standard custom, or is he letting his fancy run free? We are in two minds. We might be content to suppose the latter: that here as elsewhere in the Song, he has arranged matters to form a climax—between the kisses of passion in Song 2 and the consummation in Song 7, a night of pneumatic bliss in Song 4. Such a view would suffice, since neither we nor the poet can have access to the ways of royal harems, and imagination may have its way. But we are made to pause by the third chapter of Ruth: Ruth 'went down to the threshing-floor and did just as her mother-in-law had told her. And when Boaz had eaten and drunk, and his heart was merry, he went to lie down at the end of the heap of grain. Then she came softly, and uncovered his feet and lay down. At midnight the man was startled and turned over, and behold, a woman lay at his feet! He said, "Who are you?" And she answered, "I am Ruth your maidservant; spread your skirt over your maidservant, for you are next of kin"' (Ruth 3.6-9). The passage is famously obscure, and it has been thought that 'his feet' (*margᵉlōtāyw*) is a euphemism; the point would then be either that Naomi foresaw a chance of seducing Boaz into a premarital union, and so into a marriage with Ruth; or at least that the possibility was left open. But if a seduction were intended, surely it would be stated, and apologized for; indeed, Ruth is painted as the exemplar of humble virtue, and a seduction—or the suspicion of a seduction—would alienate the convention-bound Israelite audience. If not, we seem to be left with the presumption that a man might express his intention of marriage by spending a night with his intended, but without sexual union; and if that were so, Song 4 would seem less strange.

# Song 4

*In the Night*

3.1    At night I sought where I lay down
        My soul's beloved one—I sought,
2        But found him not—'I'll rise', I thought,
    'And comb the streets and lanes of town.
    Where has my soul's beloved been?'
3        I sought but found not; I was found
        By watchmen on the city's round—
    'My soul's beloved have you seen?'
4    I found my love—scarce did they leave me—
        My love—I caught and held him fast,
        Till to my mother's house he's passed,
    The room of her that did conceive me.
5    I put you on oath by the hinds and the roes, you daughters of
        Zion,
    Stir not love in your king, nor awaken it, till it shall please
        him.

[3.1] As 2.16f. imply, the king and the princess went to bed together, and they have been asleep, but he has woken up and left her sleeping, and gone in search of other, less limited entertainment—he has a large seraglio. She awakens and finds herself alone: the same scene recurs in 5.2ff. First (3.1) she feels for him 'on my bed'; then she decides to go out in quest of him.     [2] Just as the poet represents the audience-chamber as if it were a forest-arbour, so the palace with its corridors and spacious rooms is spoken of as a town with lanes and streets. The princess's quest is rash, but it is not implausible; and it is its rashness which shows the temper of her love.   [2b] 'I will search for him whom my soul loves'.     [3] She does not know to which of the bedrooms he may have gone—6.8 implies a minimum of 140—and cannot find him; but is found herself by the 'watchmen', that is the eunuchs, who patrol the harem to see that all is quiet. They cannot help her, and no doubt warn her to go back to bed, since the king cannot have his women behaving like this, and next time they are much more severe (5.7).

[4] 'Scarcely had I passed from them . . . ' when she finds him. 'I catch hold of him (impf.) and do not let him go till I have brought him into the house of my mother . . . ' Girls lived in their fathers' houses, not their mothers', and even if her father is dead, she has brothers (1.6): there is no biblical instance of a girl living in her 'mother's house'. The meaning is sexual. Just as at 2.4 'he brought me into the house of wine' was a euphemism for his welcoming her into his mouth, so her 'I have brought him into the house of my mother' is a euphemism for her welcoming him into her womb. 'The chamber of her who conceived me' underlines this intention. 'My mother's house' recurs with the same meaning at 8.2, and the same sexual sense underlies 8.5, where she 'awakens' him 'there where your mother conceived you'. The princess's mother is the far side of Arabia, if she is not in her grave. The princess does not mean that she immediately yields to the king; only that she takes him back to her room, and holds on to him tight till he is hers in marriage the next day. This is made clear by   [5]   , where the complaisant women of the harem are warned to keep their hooks off him until he shows he wants them. But it is also clear from the length and beauty of 4.8–5.1, which really do describe the consummation. Ancient morals were not permissive twentieth-century ways, and that went for harems too, where wives were concerned. Wives might require testimony that they had been virgins at their marriage (Deut. 22.13ff.), and the voice of the witnesses is heard immediately after the consummation of the princess's marriage, at 5.1c.

# Song 5

*The Procession*

*Chorus*

3.6 Who is this like smoking columns
                       riding up the desert way,
Clouded round with myrrh and incense,
                   all the merchant's perfum'ry?
7 Threescore mighty men escort her—
                 lo! 'tis Solomon's sedan!—
8 Of the mighty men of Israel,
                   each a seasoned veteran,
Wearing swords against the fear of
                night-time, swordsmen every man.
9 Solomon the king of Israel
                 made himself a vaulted throne,
10 Flanked about by silver pillars,
                 carved in wood of Lebanon;
On its seat a purple cushion,
                with a golden back above,
All within by Zion's daughters
                lined with leather and with love.
11 Out and see him, Zion's daughters!
                 Happy Solomon survey
In the crown his mother crowned him
                with on this his wedding day!

[3.6f.] The nuptial procession is envisaged as of the highest dignity, surrounded by clouds of incense, and with a guard of the élite of the Israelite army. Just as Lord Spencer does not bring his daughter to St Paul's Cathedral in a mere Rolls Royce, but drives with Lady Diana in a royal glass coach, so does Solomon provide his best palanquin for his bride. She ('this', *zō't*, fem.) is 'going up from the desert', that is moving northwards along the east side of Jerusalem, where the roads from Jericho and the south converge. The occasion is the king's wedding, which takes place in the open (v. 11), as weddings took place in northern Israel also, with stringed instruments from ivory palaces making the king glad (Ps. 45.8).[28] The most likely location in Jerusalem must be the extensive open ground around the Temple: the procession has left the palace and moves along the Kidron Valley in full view of the city walls, inviting the admiration of the populace. It is about to enter the Golden Gate, where the specially constructed throne stands ready. Sixty soldiers form an impressive escort, cf. sixty queens at 6.8, though not a fraction of the cortège that would accompany a king (1 Kgs 1.38, 44).

[8] 'All of them held with sword(s), instructed in war, each his sword on his thigh from the fear in the nights'. The last cannot be 'the terror by night', the pestilence of Ps. 91.5, nor the moon (Ps. 121.6), against which swords would be ineffective. They will guard the royal bedchamber from any invasion of privacy.

[9] *'appiryôn*, here rendered 'a vaulted throne', is usually translated 'palanquin', and taken to be the same as *miṭṭâ*, the sedan of v. 7. However this depends upon the highly improbable derivation from the Greek word *phoreion* (used to render it by LXX), and it robs the scene of all significance.[29] Gerleman's 'throne-room' depends on an Egyptian etymology, which is no more likely. But good—and continuous—sense is made if, with the Peshitta, the word stands for a throne with a canopy above. *'ᵃper* means a covering or bandage elsewhere in Hebrew. A. Biran uncovered the foundation of a throne at (Tel-)Dan, with four stone bases on which (?plated) wooden columns once stood, supporting such a canopy;[30] and there is evidence that it was this throne at which kings of Israel were married.[31] It stood in the open space between the outer and inner gates. [10] 'Its pillars made he of silver': these will then be the four pillars of the throne, rather than of the litter, for which they are unknown (Gerleman). 'Its *rᵉpîdâ* of gold' will be its back: *rpd* means to support, and the back is the most conspicuous part of a throne. 'Its

seat of purple' will be a cushion covered in material dyed in murex. 'Its midst is fitted with *'aha̅bâ* from the daughters of Jerusalem'. *'aha̅bâ* (normally 'love', often in the Song) seems to require a concrete meaning here, and G.R. Driver found similar words *'ih'a̅b*, hide, *'ih'ab*, soldiers' equipment, in Arabic.[32] So it is likely that the main throne structure, built of Lebanese cedar, was lined with leather on the inside. The wood and metalwork would be done by male craftsmen, the upholstering by the women—'the daughters of Jerusalem', may mean, as elsewhere, the ladies of the seraglio. But although *'aha̅bâ* thus probably means leather here, the Song is so given to double entendre, (cf. on 2.15 above) that the more normal meaning, 'love', is probably hinted also, and I have included it in the translation.

[11] 'Go out and look, daughters of Zion, on King Solomon in the crown with which his mother crowned him on the day of his wedding, and on the day of his gladness of heart'. Like a modern bridegroom, the king is awaiting the princess at the place of marriage: he is sitting in his splendid throne, and wearing a nuptial crown. Every bridegroom wore a garland or ornamental head-dress (Isa. 61.10): the king has a diadem. There may be a distinction between the 'daughters of Zion' here (only), perhaps the female inhabitants of the capital, and the 'daughters of Jerusalem' of v. 10 (and often), viz. Solomon's own women; but neither the context nor the language makes this apparent. The latter must be the speakers of the whole song, since the couple are the protagonists on the stage: and they are encouraging either one another, or the womenfolk at large, to enjoy the spectacle. The scene, and the procession preceding it, arise from the fact that 'the day of his wedding' is today; and it is of course the moment of the princess's triumph. The participation of Bathsheba, the queen-mother, or *ge̅bîrâ*, as she was known in Judah, is significant. Bathsheba was a powerful political force: Solomon owed his throne to her influence and timely action, and she was given a throne at his right hand (1 Kgs 2.19). If she crowned Solomon with a crown for his wedding to the princess, then she was giving the occasion her blessing, and the bride may hope to inherit the position of chief queen which she held under David. We have the same implication in 8.5.

# Song 6

*The Wedding*

*King*

4.1    Lo! you are fair, my friend, how fair!
       Your eyes behind your veil like doves;
   Like streaming goats your curly hair
       Down from Mount Gilead in droves.

2    Your teeth are like a sheepflock shorn;
       Up from the wash they newly swam;
   To every mother twins were born,
       And none of them has lost a lamb.

3    Your lips are like a scarlet thread,
       Your mouth delights me as it speaks;
   Like pomegranate-halves glow red
       Behind your wedding-veil your cheeks.

4    Like David's tower, whose stones in courses
       Now with a thousand shields are hung,
   The weapons of his chosen forces,
       Your neck with rows of jewels is strung.

5    Your two breasts—each is like a fawn,
       Twin offspring of a graceful deer,

6    That graze the lily-banks: till dawn
       Its breezes blow and shadows clear,

7    I'll to the hill of frankincense,
       I'll get me to the mount of myrrh.
   My friend is perfect to each sense;
       There is no blemish-spot in her.

[4.1]   The princess is wearing a veil (vv. 1, 3), which she has not been doing hitherto; and this is because she is appearing in public, for her marriage. Kings like Solomon did not expect their wives to be sullied by the stares of the plebs, and neither did their wives (Est. 1.12); but he himself can see ('Lo!'). The veil is not a yashmak with eye-slits, but is of muslin, for he can see not only her eyes, but her lips, teeth, cheeks, neck and the contour of her breasts. Her hair is 'like a flock of goats which come forth from Mount Gilead'. We can make sense of the simile only on the understanding that she has curly hair (cf. 'I am dark/black'); for just as the flock of sheep in v. 2 stands for her teeth, one sheep per tooth, so the goats cannot correspond to smooth hair, but to curly, one goat per curl. Her head, then, will be like Mount Gilead, where Jacob drove his sheep and goats (Gen. 31.23), as it is later likened to Carmel (7.5). *glš*, only here and in the same context at 6.5, means 'come into sight' in Rabbinic Hebrew.

[2]   There are 32 sheep in the flock, and the sheep are white, clearly. Lest we should think of woolly sheep, they are shorn, and lest we should think of dirty sheep, 'they have gone up from the wash'. Sheepshearing was done when the cold weather was over.[33] But the main point of the simile is that none of the bride's teeth is missing (perhaps a rarity before the days of dentists). The ewes are not mentioned here, but are implied ('all of them have had twins', 'none of them is bereaved'); they are specified in the parallel 6.6. Probably the poet has the two large incisors in mind as the ewes, with their two smaller 'lambs' alongside.   [3]   *ḥûṭ* means both a thread and a cord; the point is that the strands are twisted together at the ends of the mouth, but separable between. G takes *midbārêk* as 'talk' (*lalia*), but in both this and the subsequent laudations everything else praised is concrete and the mouth ('speaker') is meant. 'Like the cut in a pomegranate is your cheek behind your veil'. Pomegranates are hard fruits, well-coloured and often red, the size of a large apple, eaten by slitting with a knife. *plḥ* means to cut fruit in 2 Kgs 4.39, and it is likely that the comparison is with her pair of ruddy cheeks in both shape and colour.

[4]   'Your neck is like David's tower built to *talpiyyôt*'. The last word is a hapax, and is best derived from the Aramaic *lpi*, *lp'*, to arrange (Targ. Y. Lev. 6.5), Arabic *lafa'a*, to set in rows.[34] Israelite masonry was laid in rows, and towers were citadels within cities (Jg. 9.46ff), though David's tower is otherwise unknown. Towers were hung about with shields on occasions of celebration (Ezek. 27.11; 1

Macc. 4.57), such as the king's wedding day. The *gibbôrîm* are Israel's *corps d'élite*, going back to David's 'mighty men'; sixty of them are the princess's escort (3.7f.). The simile arises then from the tiers of necklaces with which the princess is adorned; Gerleman cites Egyptian illustrations as parallels, in which women wear up to ten necklaces. The masonry courses, with the shields hung down at varying heights, look like the ropes of jewels round her neck. Perhaps they include the 'necklace with links of silver' promised in 1.11.

[5ff.]   The head of a fawn, with its protuberant forehead sloping steeply down to its delicate contrasted nose, bears a close likeness to the curve of a young woman's breast, sloping down to the nipple. Now it is they, not the king that are to 'pasture in the lilies'. A number of stone lintels have been excavated in Israel, carved with the royal lily motif,[35] and looking like curling hairs; which gives the meaning both here and at 7.3. He pictures her as first lying on top of him, her breasts like the twin fawns among the hairs of his chest; and then as on her back, her perfumed breast (1.13) like two hills covered in spice-trees. Such will be the delights of their wedding-night, till the dawn-breezes. The bride is dressed for the ceremony in a long flowing robe, so he can praise her physical beauties no more, but closes the song on the general note of her perfection.

# Song 7

*The Consummation*

*King*

4.8  Come now from Lebanon with me, my bride, from Lebanon with
       me;
     Leap from the peak of Amana, the peak of Senir and Hermon,
     Down from the lioness' dens, and down from the mountains of
       leopards.
  9  Oh! You have ravished my heart, my sister, my bride!
     You have ravished my heart with one glance of your eyes, with one
       stone of your necklace!
 10  How you make love, my sister, my bride! For better your loving,
     Better than wine, and the scent of your fragrance than any spices!
 12  My sister, my bride is a garden forbidden, a mound that's forbidden,
 13  A spring that is sealed, and your runnels an Eden of pomegranates—
     Choice is the fruit, with the henna in flower, and the spikenard
       grows there,
 14  Calamus, cinnamon, saffron and nard, and the trees of incense,
     Frankincense, aloes and myrrh, and the best of all manner of
       spices—
 15  She is a garden spring, a fountain of living waters,
     Streaming from Lebanon down.
     *Princess*
           O awake, and blow through my garden,
 16  North wind and south, come both, that the fragrances stream and be
       scattered!
     Let my beloved one enter his garden and eat of his choice fruit.
     *King*
5.1  I have entered my garden, my sister, my bride; and my myrrh and
       my balsam
     Lo, I have gathered, and eaten my honeycomb steeped in its honey;
     Lo, I have drunk my wine and my milk.
     *Chorus*
     Eat to your fill, good friends, yes, drink and be drunken, good lovers!

[4.8]   The couple have not been honeymooning in the mountains, and a leap from the peak of Amana is to be recommended only for suicides! Rather we have a change of scene, and the king and his new wife are in bed together. The marriage ceremony is now over, and she can be referred to for the first time, and repeatedly, as '(my) bride'. The term comes in the present song six times, and neither before nor after; in sharp contrast to 'my friend', so regular hitherto, and clear evidence that the couple have just been married. His praise of her in the previous section ended with his resolution to betake himself to the two mountains of her breast, one of which was 'the hill of frankincense' (*l<sup>e</sup>bônâ*, whiteness); now they are named, one of them as *L<sup>e</sup>bānôn*, Mont Blanc—the bride's face may have been darkened by the Arabian sun, but her breast is of snowy whiteness. Palestine, with its little line of 3,000 ft hills, is dominated to the north by two enormous 10,000 ft ranges, Lebanon and Antilebanon, as they are known to us, Lebanon and Amana to the Israelites, with the rift valley between them. Seen from the distance they make a splendid image; nearer to, on the frontier of the land of Israel itself, are the particular peaks of the southern end of the Antilibanus range, Hermon and Senir (1 Chron. 5.23, with Baal-Hermon). The royal lover is saying that he has delighted in the 'mountains' long enough. *tāšûrî* can be derived from two different verbs *šûr*, to look, or to move, travel, leap; the meaning is given here by the association with lions and leopards, cf. Hos. 13.7, 'And I will be to them like a lion, as a leopard by the way will I leap ('*āšûr*)' (Lys). He wants them to move down, with the speed of the mountain animals.

[9]   '*<sup>a</sup>ḥōtî*, 'my sister', is a significant term of address, coming four times in this song, and again at 5.2. It is often connected with similar expressions in Egyptian love-poems, but this is only plausible in the context of widespread Egyptian links, which seem unnecessary. But Raguel calls his wife 'Sister' at Tob. 7.16, and this is more helpful: he means to address her unromantically as a fellow-member of the community of Israel. Similarly, just before, he says to Tobias, 'You are her brother (i.e. fellow-Israelite), and she is yours' (7.12). So here: with her marriage the princess has become a naturalized Israelite, a conception of central importance to the author—see below, 'A Doctrine Implied'. But despite the repetition, he has not lost his subtlety: the listener's attention is on the bride's bewitching charms—she is a sorceress who can steal away the king's heart with

her 'eye' and her (magic) stone, '$^a$naq, a jewel, as in Prov. 1.9: she has
gone to bed wearing a necklace of (?) diamonds, perhaps with a large
central stone which casts its spell. She is also wearing a nightdress
(v. 11b, *rādîd* 5.7): things have not changed much over the years.
    [10f.]   'Your loves' means physical loving throughout the Song.
The comparison to wine usually refers, as here, to kissing, which is
honey and milk under her tongue in v. 11. The fragrance is her own
fragrance, contrasted with 'all spices' here; the scent of her nightdress,
oil of cedar, is mentioned in the following verse.    [11]    refers to
intimate kissing, as in the 'chamber of wine': I have inverted the two
halves of v. 11a.
    With    [12]    the couple move towards consummating the marriage.
As a virgin bride, the princess has been barred (*nā'ûl*) or forbidden, as
an oriental garden is walled and kept locked. The image of the garden
is suggested first by the growth of hair (cf. 'my vineyard'), but is later
developed as her womb, which the king is soon to enter (4.16, 5.1).
Within the 'garden' there is a *gal*, a cairn (which does not require
emendation), her mound of Venus; and thereafter a 'spring'. The
spring is 'sealed' by the hymen.
    [13]   'Your *š$^e$lāḥîm* are a *pardēṣ* of pomegranates.' *š$^e$lāḥîm*, from
*šlḥ*, something sent, normally means missiles, and a botanical meaning,
'shoots', is usually conjectured here (cf. perhaps Ezek. 31.5). However
at Neh. 3.15 it means a conduit: 'he built the wall of the pool of the
conduit of the king's garden'—a conduit ran from early times taking
water from the Gihon spring through the city wall to the pool by the
royal garden. With this fact familiar to the revisers of Nehemiah, and
with the close correspondence of image to anatomical fact throughout,
there can be little doubt that conduits, not 'shoots', are intended: the
thought of the spring at the end of v. 12 has carried the poet's mind
on to the runnels of v. 13. The plurals are for delicacy. *pardēṣ* is a
borrowed Persian word for a royal park, or orchard, used in the LXX
for the Garden of Eden, Paradise; and makes a second evocative
image for the princess's 'garden' of delight. At the head of the
'conduit' is the cervix, a firmfleshed protuberance round which the
vagina broadens ('like a rounded cup', 7.2), with a small depression in
the centre for the cervical canal; it bears a striking resemblance,
when one comes to think of it, with the end of a pomegranate, which
is similarly curved, firm, and with a depression.[36] The same association is made with pomegranates in 8.2. All the other plants in the
garden are valued for their scent, and do not in fact grow in Israel.

The spice-plants, and even more the incense-trees with their dripping resins, symbolize her desire for her husband. She is melting with passion for him, and her fragrances (cf. v. 10) tell him so. We have had henna, (spike)nard and myrrh in 1.12f.; myrrh and aloes are aphrodisiac scents used to anoint the royal bridegroom of Ps. 45.8.

[15]   Heb. lacks 'She is . . .': the thought is resumed from v. 12. The standard 'living', i.e. running, waters now have added force: she is flooding with desire. Only in northern Israel, on the slopes of Hermon in the Lebanon range, are considerable waterfalls to be found.

[16]   She takes up the imagery (cf. 1.8). If she is a garden of scented plants and trees, she wishes the winds to carry the fullness of the perfume to her beloved. The garden is 'his garden', and she welcomes him in. The choice fruit of the pomegranates (v. 13) is 'his choice fruit', and he is to 'eat' it. At 5.1 he enters: the gathering of the spices, the eating of the honey and the drinking of the wine and milk are all symbols of love's ecstasy—the last in kissing.

[5.1c]   Such moments are most private in our culture, but in Israel the virginity of the bride and the consummation of the marriage were of public concern (Deut. 22.13ff.), and the couple slept together inside a *ḥuppâ*, a canopy, with only an awning between them and the witnesses. The Deuteronomy passage implies that the duty of the latter is the securing and preservation of the bed-linen, 'the tokens of her virginity', but the happy sounds from within tell them already that all is well, and they utter a line of blessing. The chorus here will not be the 'daughters of Jerusalem' as elsewhere, but the king's 'comrades' and the princess's 'girls'.

# Song 8

*A Knock at the Door*

*Princess*

5.2  Asleep, my heart awakes. My love!
      Hark, 'tis his voice! I hear him knock:
*King*
  'Open, my sister, friend, my dove,
      My perfect one, the door unlock.
  My head is wet with dew, my hair
  Is soaking in the damp night air.'

*Princess*

3  'My garments have I laid aside;
      Have they been taken off in vain?
  My feet for bed are washed and dried;
      Am I to dirty them again?'
  My loved one's hand has left the latch—
  I feel my loins within me catch.

5  To open to my love I stir:
      I rise, my hands distilling nard;
  My fingers wet with liquid myrrh
      The bolt with which the door is barred.
6  I open to my dearest one—
  And lo, my love had turned and gone.

  While still he spoke my life had gone;
      I sought, but he could not be found;
  I called, but answer was there none;
7      The watchmen on the city's round,
  They found me, and they beat me sore,
  And stripped from me the robe I wore.

  The watchmen keep the city walls.
8      O daughters of Jerusalem,
  If you should find within these halls
      My dear beloved, say to him—
  Swear to me by the powers above—
  That I for him am sick with love.

*Chorus*

9  What is your love more than any beloved, O fairest of
   women?
   What is your love more than any beloved, that thus you
   adjure us?

[5.2]   The scene is not a dream, nor is it to be understood in terms
of a stock of traditional lovers' laments used playfully. It is the night
after the wedding night, or one soon succeeding. The princess has
gone to bed alone, prudently pulling the bolt (v. 5) on her bedroom
door, and gone to sleep: there is no sign that the king began the night
with her as he had at 3.1, nor could we explain his difficulty with the
door if he had. He has a large complement of women in the seraglio,
some of whom no doubt he is fond of, and his new wife cannot
sensibly expect his favours every night. However he has found her
very satisfying as a partner, and it is not long before he is back. She 'is
asleep but her heart awakes', and she recognizes that it is him, as he
calls and knocks. Her apartment faces out on to the palace garden
(2.9), and he has come to the garden door, perhaps for privacy. 'My
head is filled with dew, My locks with the drops of the night'. I have
added 'the door unlock'.
   [3]   'I have taken off my shift; how shall I put it on? I have washed
my feet; how am I to dirty them?' She is not being playful or
coquettish: he means too much to her. She is just bleary-eyed and
half asleep, and nature expresses itself in excuses. But with   [4]
things change: 'My loved one put forth his hand from the hole; and
my inward parts were moved upon me/him'. The hole is the hole in
the door through which the latch passes: it is not a euphemism, or we
should not be able to make sense of the following lines. Gerleman
thinks the young man has put his hand 'through' the hole, but *min*
does not mean 'through' (even at 2.9). It is better to think with
Gordis that what gets the princess moving is the realization that he
has *withdrawn* his hand (cf. 1 Kgs 13.4a) from the latch-hole, and so
is moving away. *šālaḥ*, like its English counterpart 'to send', usually

means sending from where you are, as when Mrs Thatcher sent the fleet from England to the Falklands; but it is also possible to send from elsewhere, as when she sent a second fleet from Gibraltar, and this is what the king is doing here. *mē'îm*, the inward parts, are often used for the centre of the emotions, which the Israelites located physically: 'were moved' could be of any emotion, here chiefly love and fear (of losing him). BHS prints 'upon him', but many Hebrew MSS and the Targum have the harder 'upon me' (but cf. Ps. 42.4); the meaning is not affected.

[5]    Fearing, with good reason, that her slow response has caused him to withdraw, she gets up and goes to open the door. 'My hands distilled myrrh, and my fingers liquid myrrh upon the hoops of the bolt': just as her lips distilled sweet nectar, and her tongue honey and milk, in the last scene (4.11), so now her hands become clammy with perspiration, and her fingers with the bitter 'myrrh' of the sweat of anxiety. With damp and trembling touch she slides back the bolt.

[6]    Her fears were only too well justified: the end of the king's tapping on the latch-hole was indeed a sign that he had 'turned and gone'.

[6b]    repeats the desolate discovery. *napšî* normally 'my soul' = me; but no good sense is given by 'While he spoke, my soul went forth', for while he was speaking she was far from despair, terror, etc. Both here and (even more clearly) at 6.12 the phrase refers to the king, and is an endearment, like the Italian 'vita mia': he did not wait while she was lingering in bed, but left as soon as he had finished speaking—which is why his hand had left the latch. She goes after him as in 3.1ff., but this time it becomes clear what risk she incurs by her rash devotion.    [7]    The king must have order in his harem, and cannot have wild women circulating in the place shrieking. We have met 'the watchmen on the city's round' before, the eunuchs, in 3.3; and this time they ensure discipline with a whip. 'They beat me, they wounded me': *pš'* implies that they drew blood, though it will not perhaps have been very severe in view of what follows.[37] Although the poet mentions the removal of her *rādîd* after the beating, there is no suggestion of her being naked thereafter (cp. 6.6), and the order of events should be understood as reversed. The *rādîd* is a delicate garment (Isa. 3.23), and will have been her nightdress, and all she was wearing. There is irony in the last phrase, 'keepers of the walls': the eunuchs' business is to keep outsiders from the harem, rather than beating a defenceless girl for loving her husband.

[8]   The palace women once more provide the opportunity for a change of scene. 'I adjure you . . . what you are to say to him: that I am sick with love': the message is not that she has been whipped, but that she is heart-broken. The ladies are not only extraordinarily accommodating, but are conveniently about in the middle of the night.

[9]   Lys thinks the Chorus's comment is bitter and ironic, 'What is your sweetheart, fairest of women?' This may be right, as there was a similar ironic touch at 1.8, 'Follow the track . . .'; but the poet's purpose is to form a transition to the next scene, where the questions are answered on the level.

# Song 9

*A Lover Lost and Found*

*Princess*

5.10 My love is of a ruddy cheer;
    None of ten thousand is his peer.

11 His head is gold unalloyed, where
    Like palm-flowers curls his raven hair;

12 His eyes like doves by waters cool,
    Milk-washed, that nest beside a pool;

13 His bearded cheeks a balsam-bed,
    With garden-herbs banked overhead;
    His lips are lilies as it were,
    Distilling drops of liquid myrrh;

14 His hands are cylinders of gold,
    Which jaspers at their tips enfold;
    His loins a tusk of ivory,
    Inlaid with lapis lazuli;

15 His legs are marble columns set
    On golden bases for his feet.
    In form he stands like Lebanon,
    Choice as the cedars thereupon;

16 Within his mouth is sweetness' height,
    And all of him is pure delight.
    I love and company with him,
    O daughters of Jerusalem.

*Chorus*

6.1 Where is he gone, your beloved, O fair among women?
    Where has he turned, your beloved one, that we may help
           you to find him?

*Princess*

2 Down to his garden my loved one has gone, to the beds of
           balsam,
    There in the gardens to pasture, and gather the lilies.

                                  [Enter King

3 I am my love's, my beloved is mine—he that feeds in the
    lilies!

[5.10] 'My love is glowing and ruddy, conspicuous above ten thousand': the ruddy glow is a sign of health. The same root is used of the attractive young David in 1 Sam. 16.12. As with the king's praise of the princess in ch. 4, she begins at the top and moves downwards.

[11] 'His head is gold (of) pure gold': the syntactical relationship between the two words for gold is not quite clear, but the image relates to the colour of his skin—he is a pleasant brown, cf. his golden fingers in v. 14 and his golden feet in v. 15. 'His locks are *taltallîm*, black as the raven'. *taltallîm* occur only here in the Bible. They may be related to the Akkadian *taltallu*, the black panicle of the date-palm, with which the hair is sometimes compared in Arabic poetry; but in rabbinic Hebrew it means curls, locks.     [12] 'by water brooks'. The eyes are, as usual, doves, that is, the eye-lids are like a pair of fan-tails going up and down, and so 'bathing' in the milk of the iris. The doves are said to be dwelling by a fullness (*millē't*): N.H. Tur-Sinai cites Gen. R. 95 (ed. Theodor), where the word means a pool,[38] and this gives good sense both for the image in general, and as a reference to the dark, brimming surface of the pupil. The water-brooks are the tear-ducts close by.     [13] 'His cheeks are like a bed of balsam-trees, *migdᵉlôt* of spices'. The king, like Aaron in Ps. 133.2, has precious ointment running down his beard, so that it seems like a plantation of aromatic trees. The *migdᵉlôt* of spices are not towers, but terraced beds on a higher bank: his beard has a moustache above. 'His lips are lilies distilling liquid myrrh'—lilies are suggested, as elsewhere, by their deep calyx and glorious scent. No colour is mentioned, in contrast to much of the rest of the song, though red or purple lilies are often supposed. In ch. 4 the bride's lips distilled nectar, which would be more suitable for lilies, but the poet prefers myrrh for its liquidity, echoing 5.5.

[14] The golden *gᵉlîlê* are the fingers of the king's hands, which are 'filled with *taršiš*'. *gālîl* means a cylinder, sometimes quite small, a swivel-pin in a door-hinge (1 Kgs 6.34, NEB). *taršiš* is an undefined semi-precious stone, often yellow or tawny in colour: jasper in Ezek. 1.16, Gk. *chrysolithos*. It could be that his fingers are covered in jewelled rings, but elsewhere the praise is entirely of his body, not its accoutrements, and probably his nails are in mind. The opaque jasper, or the pink form of beryl would be suitable.     [14b] See discussion in Introduction.     [15] 'His legs are columns of marble set on bases of gold': marble, from its veining, and its preciousness. It is used for both columns and flooring of different colours in Ahasuerus'

palace (Est. 1.16). The exposed parts of the king's body, face, hands
and feet, are all gold. [15b]    'His form is like Lebanon, choice as the
cedars'. *mar'eh* is used for the whole body, as with the princess in
2.14; he is royal in height, like Lebanon, or (thought association) the
tall cedars of Lebanon.     [16]    'His mouth is sweetness, and all of
him is delight': *ḥēk* is the palate, and it is his kisses that taste so sweet
(1.2; 2.4; 7.10). She ends her sad description of her lost lover, 'This is
my beloved and this my companion, daughters of Jerusalem': the
restraint and irony of 'my companion' give the passage dignity and
pathos.

[6.1]    The plaintive scene ends, as often, with the chorus's reply:
where has the king gone 'that we may seek him with you?' Lys again
suspects irony.

[2]    She knows full well. 'His garden', which symbolized her
moment of ecstasy at 4.16, now means his seraglio, where other
blossoms flower. His cheeks, with their perfumed hair, were a 'bed of
balsam' at 5.13: now he has 'gone down', as he did from Lebanon and
Amana at 4.8, to other 'beds', perfumed with the scent of other
women. He is in fresh woods and 'pastures' new; in the gardens—
now plural, cf. 4.12ff.—and picking other lovely lilies (cf. 2.1f., 16).
The use of phrases which have so far been symbols of her own
happiness strikes a note of high pathos.

[3]    Up to 6.2 she has been seeking the lost king in vain, with or
without the comfort of the palace women. From 6.4 he is praising her
once more, and at 6.11 they are again making love: so somewhere
between 6.2 and 6.4 he must make his appearance. Verse 3 is her cry
of triumph, as it was at 2.16, and will be again at 7.10: so he must
have appeared after 6.2. His arrival tells her that all is well: he has
found no satisfaction in his other balsam-beds, and has come back to
her. 'He who pastures in the lilies' has returned to his own lily among
the thorns.

# Song 10

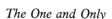

*The One and Only*

*King*

6.4 Ah! You are beautiful, my friend,
    Like Tirzah on a summer's day,
As lovely as Jerusalem,
    As awesome as the Milky Way.

5 Oh, turn away your eyes from me;
    They dazzle me, they make me mad:
Your hair runs as a herd of goats
    Comes streaming down from Gilead.

6 Your teeth are like a ewe-flock washed,
    Each with her twins, and none bereft,
And underneath your veil your cheeks
    Are like a pomegranate cleft.

8 Though I have eighty concubines,
    And sixty queens beside the throne,
And virgin girls untold; my dove,
9     My perfect one, she stands alone.
Alone her mother's shining joy,
    All women saw and called her blessed;
The very queens and concubines
    Their praises thus to her addressed:

10 'Oh, who is this that looks from out
    Her window like the dawn of day,
Fair as the moon, bright as the sun,
    As awesome as the Milky Way?'

*Princess*

11 I went down to the garden of nuts, to look on the shoots of
    the valley,
To see if the vine was in bud, and the pomegranates were
    flowering:

12 Ere I had thought it, he made me, my life did, my own
    people's chariot,
Come from Nadiv.

[6.4] 'You are beautiful, my friend, as Tirzah, lovely as Jerusalem, awesome as the *nidgālôt*'. The king confesses the princess's supremacy in his love. He opens by restating his admiration for her beauty, and in vv. 5-7 repeats, with some modifications and abbreviations, his praises of 4.1-4. But this time he is not content just to admire, and to desire (4.6): the point now is that she outshines all his harem (vv. 8f.), and is agreed so to do by common consent (vv. 9f.). He compares her first to the two capital cities of tenth-century Israel, Jeroboam's capital at Tirzah in the northern kingdom, and Jerusalem in Judah. Tirzah is preferred to Samaria, the later and more famous capital of northern Israel, because the latter was not yet built in Solomon's time; Tirzah is presumed to have been a fair city already, for Jeroboam to have chosen it for his national centre, though not so fair as Jerusalem, which is placed after it in crescendo. Ancient cities, with carefully designed walls and palaces, were beautiful as modern cities are not, and are elsewhere compared to a bride (Isa. 54.6; Rev. 21.2), or to other kinds of woman (Ezek. 16; 23).

The *nidgālôt* are a standing problem. We have met *degel*, a standard, at 2.4, and *dagal* means to set up a standard at Ps. 20.7; but we have also seen the king described as *dāgûl*, conspicuous, at 5.10, and a second verb is often supposed, meaning to see. Thus *nidgālôt* by derivation could mean 'bannered ones' or 'seen ones' (feminine passive participle). It occurs twice in this song (only), once following Tirzah and Jerusalem, once (6.10) following the dawn, the moon and the sun. Now the problem consists in this. It is unexampled in the Song for the poet to flit from one field of imagery to another in the same sentence: what then is there that would make a third member to both the sequence, Tirzah, Jerusalem . . . , and the sequence, the moon, the sun . . . ? Furthermore we have been led to expect something in the nature of a climax by the poet's writing elsewhere—e.g. the flowers, the singing, the turtledove, or the garden fountain, the well of living water, the streams from Lebanon: and here Tirzah seems to lead up to Jerusalem, and the moon to the sun. The answer seems to be the constellations, a suggestion already made by W. Rudolph;[39] for they are the third (and only possible) member of the regular trio, the sun, the moon and the stars, and the thought of the heavens as a city is biblical also.

The latter idea is old, and has its roots in Joseph's dream in Gen. 37, where the sun and moon and the eleven 'stars' (constellations) bow before Joseph's 'star'; so that the twelve tribes have their counterpart in the heavens. More concretely, the Tabernacle is modelled on the pattern of its heavenly counterpart, which God shows to Moses in heaven (Exod. 25.9; etc.). This is then built and used for worship by the twelve tribes in the early chapters of Numbers, each drawn up under its *degel*, standard, round its four sides. We see thus in process of development the notion of Israel as the earthly antitype of the constellations in heaven; and it reaches its clear conclusion in Rev. 21, where the Lamb's bride is the holy city Jerusalem coming down from heaven, with twelve gates on which are inscribed the names of the twelve tribes of Israel. So *nidgālôt* means 'Bannered Ones', i.e. the twelve constellations each with its (proto-) zodiacal sign. As the stars may exercise a fatal influence on human life (Jg. 5.20), they are spoken of as 'awesome': note the transition of the adjectives in moving from the earthly cities to the heavenly one— 'fair, lovely, awesome'.

[5] In 4.1 the king praised his bride's eyes as like doves; but at 4.9 she was a sorceress, stealing his heart with one of her eyes, and now she is not merely beautiful but awesome, and her eyes 'disturb' him. He is under their spell, and asks her to turn them away. [5b-7] repeat almost verbatim 4.1c-3. The flock is this time expressly of ewes, and their shearing is omitted; Gilead is no longer 'Mount' Gilead, and her lips are left out. Of the features described, the first, her hair (*ša'rēk*), is probably also thought of as being dangerous, the word being related to *šā'îr*, a demon (hairy one). But the rest seems to be mere repetition, and this has its price. In ch. 4 the princess was being married in public, and was wearing a veil. It is difficult to think of any reason why she should be veiled inside the palace, and vv. 11f. imply that the end of the scene takes place not even before the women, but in bed. 'Behind your veil' seems therefore to be an unintended carryover from the earlier context, one of the Song's rare failures to think precisely.

[8f.] 'There are sixty queens and eighty concubines, and virgins without number: my dove, my perfect one, she is one. One was she to her mother, shining to her that bore her.' The count of palace women is much less than in 1 Kgs 11.3; Solomon is taken to be still young, perhaps, but the competition is considerable. The queens come first in Heb., making a climax in number against an anticlimax in status; so also in v. 9, 'her mother . . . daughters . . . the queens and concubines', whose admiration is the most surprising of all. This is the only passage referring to Israelite queens, though the word is used of foreign queens, e.g. of Sheba or Persia. They are normally called the king's 'wives', and in Israel, as elsewhere,[40] there was one who held the pre-eminence, Bathsheba, Maacah and Jezebel for example.

[9b] 'Daughters saw and called her blessed', cf. Leah's words at the birth of Asher, 'Daughters will call me blessed' (Gen. 30.13). From their place in the sequence the 'daughters' could conceivably be the 'virgins' of v. 8. The use of the verb 'praise', the comparison with the luminaries, and the situation of all looking up to the princess in her window, combine to make the suggestion of divinity: so too the repeated 'One is she . . . ', rather reminiscent of the confession that Yahweh is one.     [10]   'Who is this that looks out . . . ?' 'Who is this . . . ?' marks public recognition several times in the Song, cf. 3.6, 8.5. *nišqāpâ*, looking out, is often used as from a window, e.g. Jg. 5.28, 2 Sam. 6.16. The king's praise closes in a lovely climax which recalls its opening: 'You are *fair*, my friend (v. 4) . . . *Shining* was she to her that bore her (v. 9) . . . *Awesome* as the Bannered Ones (v. 4)'. The words for moon and sun are abnormal: *l<sup>e</sup>bānâ*, the White One, and *ḥammâ*, the Heat, both perhaps in reference to her colouring. She is dark, but fair as the pale moon, and bright as the scorching sun.

[11]   She has won the king's love by her beauty and by her perseverance, and they are alone together once more. He has just been down to 'his gardens', 'pasturing' with his other women; and she 'goes down' to see if his strength has returned. The 'garden of nuts' carries the same symbolism as the apples and figs: walnuts are common in Palestine, and are borne in pairs. *naḥal* means a water-course or valley, where the fresh growth first pushes its way up: the shooting of the greenery, and of the vine-buds, stands for his rising desire, to which, indeed, the pomegranate-flower bears an almost embarrassing likeness. Verse 12 has for long been a riddle, but the context gives the sense. To her surprise, he is ready: 'I had not known (but) . . . ' *napší*, lit. 'my life', means 'my love' again, as at 5.6, and forms the natural syntax as the subject of the feminine verb *sāmat<sup>e</sup>nî*, 'my life set me'. *mark<sup>e</sup>bôt 'ammî*, ' . . . as the chariots of my people', is an echo from earlier in the Song. When first he saw her, the king compared the princess to his mare in the chariots (*rik<sup>e</sup>bê*) of Pharaoh (1.9): now, she says, he has made her a chariot of her own people— that is, she is still the mare, but he is now the 'charioteer'. The Hebrews had thus already discovered that sexual union could take place in more than one position. The verse ends with the word *nadîb*, which is joined to *'ammî* with a hyphen in the Heb.: hence the

'chariots of Amminadib/ab' of the translations. But the word recurs at 7.2, where *bat-nadîb* suggests that her people is called Nadiv, and that the hyphen is an ancient indication that the words should be taken so: the expression can mean 'daughter of Nadiv' as easily as 'daughter of a prince'. 1 Chron. 5.19 speaks of two Arabian tribes called Naphish and Nodab (Gr. *Nadabaioi*), and LXX renders 7.2 'daughter of Nadab'; so there is not much difficulty in supposing that she came from a north Arabian tribe of this name. Cf. too 1.5, the tents of Kedar.

# Song 11

*The Dance*

*Chorus*
7.1 Come back, come back, O Shulammite, show us your countenance!
*Princess*
Look not upon the Shulammite as on a choral dance.

[Dances]

*King*
2 O sandaled daughter of Nadiv, how beautiful your feet!
    Your thighs are turned like jewels made to exquisite design;
3     Your womb a rounded chalice—may it lack not mingled wine!—
Your belly is of lily-flowers beside a mound of wheat.

4 Your breasts are like a pair of fawns, twin offspring of a deer;
5     Your neck a tower of ivory, so tall and fair you seem;
    Your eyes are pools in Heshbon by the gate of Bath-Rabbim;
Your nose is like Mount Lebanon above Damascus sheer.

6 Your head is like to Carmel with the forests on its brow;
    Your hair is rich as purple, and its ringlets bind the king.
7     How fair, how sweet you are! 'Tis love these gracefulnesses
        bring.
8 You're tall as is a palm, your breasts are clusters by its bough.

9 I'll clamber up the palm, I thought, I'll grasp its fruit like reapers;
    Then be, my sweet, your breasts to me as clusters of the vine,
10     Your nostrils' breath like apples and your mouth like vintage
        wine—

*Princess*
To touch my love's erectness, and my lips to kiss his sleepers!

[7.1-10 (EVV 6.13–7.9)] presents a new sequence, the chorus once more providing the transition. The plot moves forward. In ch. 6 the princess has established her attraction for the king as overwhelming: but has this not been achieved rather easily—what about his former favourites?

[1] suggests some competition. David's last days had been comforted by the 'very fair damsel' Abishag the Shunammite, and she passed over into Solomon's harem (1 Kgs 2.17ff.). As the town of Shunem is called Solem or Sulam today,[41] the (traditional) reference to Abishag is extremely likely: our oldest manuscript, the Greek Vaticanus, has *Soumaneitis*.[42] The chorus calls, 'Come back, come back, O Shulammite; come back, come back that we may look on you'—she is so lovely. This draws an active response from our heroine who has no intention of being upstaged: 'Why will you look...?' = 'Look not...', as at 8.4. *kim<sup>e</sup>hôlat hammah<sup>a</sup>nāyim*, 'like the dance of the two companies'. The reference is lost to us, but it is plausible that one of the big spectacles of palace life was a festival dance with a double chorus of dancers. The place Mahanaim was called after the two companies of angels seen by Jacob (Gen. 32.2).

The king's praise of the princess in the following verses suggests strongly that she now dances for him herself. (a) He begins from her feet, and specifies her sandals. (b) The comparison to a palm-tree in vv. 8f. makes good sense only if her arms are being waved aloft like palm-branches (v. 9a). (c) The description is more explicit than in earlier praises, suggesting that she is either naked or dressed in diaphanous veils, both of which conditions were probably normal in palace dancing. The impression seems to be confirmed by the reference to the dance of the two companies: just as 'our bed' (1.16) soon implies that she is lying on it (2.6), so the mention of a dance here leads on to action suited to the word.

[2] Whereas the praises in chs. 4, 5 and 6 have all begun from the head and moved downwards, the movement is in reverse here. 'How beautiful are your feet in sandals, O daughter of Nadiv': Vaticanus has 'daughter of Nadab', and supports the suggestion above (6.12) that Nadiv is her home. 'The turnings of your thighs are like jewels, the work of the hands of a craftsman'. *hammûqê*, from *hmq*, to turn (5.6), could of itself refer either to the whirling movements of her legs in the dance, or their curves. But the simile shows that the second is right: *h<sup>a</sup>lā'îm* are jewels or ornaments (Prov. 25.12), and are said to be the work of an artist-workman.

[3] 'šor°rēk is a rounded cup—may it never lack mixed wine.' šōr comes twice elsewhere in the Bible: it means a navel-string at Ezek. 16.4, and some inner part of a man (par. 'bones') at Prov. 3.8. LXX renders 'navel', perhaps from the cup simile; but there is no basis for this in Heb., or any other Semitic language, while sirr(i) in Arabic means 'secret', and is used for venereal (diseases). It may be an equivalent for mē'îm in Prov. 3, and, as Lys says about Ezek. 16, the navel-string goes to the womb as well as the navel. This is clearly the meaning here. The entrance to the womb is shaped like a rounded cup, the vagina being at first like the thin stem, and then broadening out into a hemispherical bowl round the cervix ('pomegranate'). There would be no equivalent for 'mixed wine' in the navel, but the intoxicating juices of the womb were a theme of the Consummation song: indeed here the mention of mezeg, wine mixed with spices to make it more heady, and the jussive—'may it never lack . . . '—show that the king has mingling of another sort in mind. Furthermore, the poem is moving up the body, and the womb comes before the belly, the navel naturally after. 'Your belly is a mound of wheat edged with lilies'. Flat tummies are more generally admired today, and we should probably think of her as executing a belly-dance: but tastes change, and Botticelli's Venus (let alone Rubens' heroines) warns against confidence in such matters. The lilies are the curling hairs on its lower side, as at 4.5.

[4] As the princess is erect and dancing, her breasts resemble the twin fawns again: lying, they are mountains.  [5] The tower of ivory simile does not mean that her neck is white (since she is 'black', 1.5f., this would be unlikely). There are 'ivory palaces' at Ps. 45.8, and 'houses of ivory' at Am. 3.15 and 1 Kgs 22.39, and these were not white either, but were decorated with ivories within, and were a mark of royal dignity and distinction (and extravagance). The image is a variant of 'the tower of David' at 4.4, and signifies 'tall and fair' (which are my interpretation, and not in the Heb.). The topography of Heshbon is unknown to us: perhaps the pools lay to left and right of the gate leading to a (now forgotten) village, Bath-Rabbim, as her eyes are to either side of her nose.  [5c] The ancients did not admire enormous noses any more than we do. The parallel is with the steep fallaway of (Anti-)Lebanon on the east side facing Damascus, not its height. 'Your nose is like the peak of Lebanon looking towards Damascus': migdāl, a 'highness', often a tower, is probably used for the natural peak, as it is used for the 'banks' at 5.13.

[6] 'Your head upon you is like Carmel.' Nearer home, and not so grandiose, is the comparison with Carmel, which also falls away steeply, above Haifa: *rō'š* means both 'head' and '(mountain-)top'. The likeness extends to the woods which still cover the escarpment and so parallels both her brow and her hair. *karmîl*, purple shellfish, were named after Carmel where they were fished, and lead on to the thought of the next line: 'And the *dallat* of your head is like purple: the king is bound in the *rᵉhāṭîm*'. *dallāh* is the thrum, the fringe of unwoven threads that hang down *(dll)* at the edge of a woven fabric; cf. Isa. 38.12, 'Like a weaver have I rolled up my life; thou hast cut me off from the *dallâ*'. These are often taken to be long threads, like the princess's supposed long hair, but a short fringe is just as likely. It is purple in being dark and lustrous, a colour sometimes suggested today by the light on the hair of Asian women,⁴³ and consists of *rᵉhāṭîm*. Elsewhere these are troughs for watering animals (Gen. 30.38, 41; Exod. 2.16), and the imaginative link is probably with the curls in her hair, which have been referred to before (4.1; 6.5), and are like little basins. It is however possible that the word was also used as a technical term in weaving, weaving-rings perhaps; it could be with the thought of Samson in mind, who was bound by Delilah by the hair on to a loom (Jg. 16.13f.). In any case the round shape of the curls suggests the image of the links of a chain, and the king is 'bound', captivated by them.

[7] The first half of the verse is addressed to the princess, and the second should therefore mean 'love is in daintinesses'. He means, 'Dainty, graceful features displayed in your dancing move me to love'; and this provides the transition to the last section of the lyric, and its point. She is not just beautiful; she moves him to love, and he desires her.    [8]   'This your stature is like a palm, and your breasts like clusters': her tall, graceful figure and raised arms, waving in dance like a palm-tree bending in the wind, make him think of her breasts as like the clusters of dates growing on the stem where the fronds begin.

[9] The thought now moves to action. As the harvester of dates must shin up the tall, rough trunk to gain the fruit, so will he climb on his beloved and delight in her breasts: 'I said, I will climb in the palm, I will take hold of its panicles: And let your breasts, pray, be as vine-clusters'. His mind goes from the palm-clusters to the even more delicious grape clusters; and so to other fruit images. Her breasts will taste as sweet as grapes; her breath will smell as pleasant

as apples with their fresh scent. Gerleman suggests that Israelite couples kissed with their noses as well as in other ways, as did Egyptians; but the kissing in any case soon moves to her mouth, where her palate (*ḥēk*) tastes like the best wine (2.4; etc.).

[10] The meaning is intentionally obscure. MT has 'And your palate like the best wine, going for my beloved to *mêšārîm*, uprightness, gliding over the lips of the sleepers'; but no good sense can be made of this, and I will suggest that a small change in the vowels has been made to avoid indecency.

'Your palate' has a feminine suffix, and therefore refers to the princess, while 'my beloved' in the Song always means the king: so he is still the speaker down to 'wine', and these words belong with v. 9, while she takes over from 'Going...' This is generally agreed. However the two participles, 'going', 'gliding', could refer either to the wine or to the princess's mouth: it is usual to take the wine as the subject ('gliding over the lips...'), but this has not been a fruitful option, and it is better to consider the alternative. We have two further complications. First, *mêšārîm*, from *yšr*, straight, upright, is a plural-form abstract noun, normally meaning 'uprightness' in a moral sense (15x); it also means 'levelness' at Isa. 26.7, and it is used of wine 'going in smoothness' at Prov. 23.31, through this is suspected of being an introduction from our passage.[44] But a physical, sexual meaning has also been suggested for our verse,[45] and this would give good sense in line with the playful eroticism which we have found throughout the poem. He says, 'Your mouth is like wine' with its kisses: yes, she replies daringly, 'It goes to my beloved to his "uprightness"'.

But what about 'the lips of the sleepers'? *yᵉšēnîm*, 'sleepers', is a plural noun that looks as if it were in some way in parallel with *mêšārîm*, and the meanings, upright/sleeping, could easily be some form of contrast. This raises the suggestion that the lips of the second half of the line could be in parallel with 'your mouth' in the first; and it is at this point that our second complication comes in. The Hebrew consonants *śpty* can be given more than one set of vowels. The MT reads *śipᵉtê*, 'the lips of', but the Greek translators took the word as *śᵉpātay*, 'my lips'; and although LXX's deviations from MT are not usually a cause for confidence, in this case 'my lips' makes an excellent parallel with 'your mouth', and provides clear and characteristic sense. 'Your mouth is intoxicating', says the king: 'it goes', replies the princess with a twinkle, to my beloved's 'uprights', it glides with my lips over his 'sleepers'. It is no surprise that the Hebrew tradition has obscured these delicate euphemisms with its alignments and vocalization; or that the Song was treated with caution as leading to lust. But the meaning is really quite plain from the consonants, and it is a sense entirely in line with the subtle eroticism of the whole poem; indeed it is carried further in 8.2, in the following song.

# Song 12

*A Night in the Country*

*Princess*

7.11  I am my love's, his desire is for me! O come, my beloved,

12  Let us away to the country; the night we can sleep in the henna.

13  Early we'll be to the vineyards and see if the vines have sprouted,

Whether their blossoms are out, and the pomegranate is flowering.

14  There will I give you my love: for the mandrakes are shedding their fragrance,

And at our doors will be fruits, all manner of fruit in perfection,

New ones and old, which I have made ready for you, my beloved!

8.1  I wish you were my brother,
And sucked my mother's breast;
I'd find and kiss you in the street,
And no one would protest.

2  I'd take you to my mother's,
To drink my spiced wine—
You'd show me how—and taste the sweet
Of pomegranate mine.

3  Under my head will his left hand be, and his right will enfold me.

4  I put you on oath that you stir not love, you daughters of Zion,

Stir not love in your king, nor awaken it till it shall please him.

[7.11]   The dance has brought the princess's triumph: she has eclipsed even the beautiful Abishag. It is she that the king desires, and she capitalizes her advantage. As long as he merely visits her in her room, as in chs. 4–5, she is on a par with any of the other women. What she wants is a unique and public position, to be Queen, because she loves him (8.6), as well as for any more worldly motives.

[12]   So she suggests that they go out into the country, and spend the night sleeping among the henna blossom. $k^e p\bar{a}r\hat{i}m$ could mean 'villages', but it meant henna at 4.13; and henna scent is beautiful, and erotic (4.13), while an ancient village hostel is likely to have been dirty and sordid.

[13]   They can be awake at dawn and sleep together in the open amid the scents of May. We have noted throughout the double-entendre of the vineyard, representing her sexually; and she hints delicately that they will see whether his 'desire is for her' then. The sprouting vineshoots opening their blossom-buds, and the pomegranate-flower with its long, tubular corolla, are alike symbols of his desire, as at 6.11.

[14]   There, she says, shall nature and human love be at one. The mandrake ($d\hat{u}d\bar{a}$', the love apple) bears highly scented, golden-yellow fruit in the late spring: Reuben found mandrakes in the 'country' ($\acute{s}\bar{a}deh$) at the time of wheat-harvest (Pentecost), and brought them to his mother as an aphrodisiac (Gen. 30.14ff.). As the mandrakes flood the air with their scent, so will the princess's fragrance as she 'gives him her love' ($d\bar{o}day$, a play on words).

[14b]   The imagery alters a little. In vv. 13-14a the couple have been lying in the peace and seclusion of the country vineyard: now there are 'doors', and fruit which she has made ready by them. The human reality has taken over from the natural symbolism. The door is used as a sexual euphemism in Talmudic Hebrew. It is the gate into the forbidden Eden of 4.12, and the 'fruit in perfection' ($m^e g\bar{a}d\hat{i}m$, the 'choice fruit' of 4.13, 15) is the delight of sexual union. Gerleman is probably right is taking 'doors' as a generalizing plural, though 'our doors' could refer to them both. But the 'fruit' has been prepared by her alone: it is 'new and old'—some paths to love's ecstasy they have shared already, others she has yet to show him.

[8.1]   She wants the freedom to love her husband openly; partly because of the strength of her feelings, which have just been so eloquently expressed; and partly because of her related hope of becoming his publicly recognized consort. But such lack of restraint is acceptable only in children; if she behaved like this she would be 'despised' (*yābûzû*) as a whore (Prov. 7.13).    [2]  'I would lead you, I would bring you to my mother's house. You would instruct me: I would give you to drink of spiced wine, of the juice of my pomegranate.' The innocent scene of the child sister taking her elder brother home for a drink of wine with spices and some pomegranate juice conceals a further erotic double entendre. *'eššoq<sup>e</sup>kā*, I would kiss you, in v. 1 leads on by assonance to *'ašq<sup>e</sup>kā*, I would give you to drink. The sexual meaning is not in doubt. We have met 'the house of my mother', meaning the womb, before at 3.4; the 'wine of spices' sounds very like the mingled wine in the 'chalice' of 7.2 (though wine has also often referred to kisses); 'my pomegranate' recalls 'my vineyard that is mine' of 1.6 and 8.12, and the 'paradise of pomegranates', the 'garden' of 4.13. The only question is what sort of sexual activity is envisaged. We may think of straightforward sexual union. This is symbolized by drinking at the climax of the Consummation, at 5.1, 'I drink my wine with my milk'; and it may fairly be said that if his left hand is to be under her head (8.3), the logistic possibilities will be rather limited. On the other hand, we have to consider the alternative that the 'drinking' is meant literally. At 7.9 he was thinking to taste her breasts like grape-clusters; at 7.10 she promised to stimulate him orally, her mouth 'going to his uprightness'; at 7.13 she spoke of fruits 'new and old' at her 'doors', and it is not likely that the hope of new fruits is brought in to be disappointed. It seems probable then that she is speaking here of oral sex on his side,[46] as a preamble to the full union of 8.3 (celebrated at v. 5b). This is confirmed by the otherwise mysterious *t<sup>e</sup>lamm<sup>e</sup>dēnî*, which could mean either 'she ... ' or 'you would instruct me'. In the children's idyll, mother could show the girl how to squeeze the pomegranates; but this would have no point in the underlying erotic scene. On the other hand, the audience might well wonder how the princess, as a virgin bride, could come to know about such practices: she doesn't, replies the poet, she has only heard about them; but he is an experienced husband and he will show her how. This could only be the case if what was being spoken of were an untried delight, a new fruit; they have enjoyed the old fruits together twice already.

[3]   She looks forward to his making love to her in the country, with a reprise of 2.6.    [4]   Now she must go and make ready, and for the last time puts the women on oath not to tempt the king in her absence. Perhaps this is hardly necessary, but forms the transition into the penultimate scene.

# Song 13

*Love's Demand*

*Chorus*

8.5  Who is this whose love supports her coming up the desert
       way?

*Princess*
      Under the apple tree did I awaken you,
      There where your mother conceived you in ecstasy,
      Where she who bore you conceived in her ecstasy.

6   Make me the seal upon your heart,
      The seal upon your hand as well;
  For love, my sweet, is strong as death,
      And jealousy is hard as hell.

7   The mighty seas cannot avail
      To quench the flames of love's desire,
  Nor all the floods suffice to drown
      Its blaze divine of lightning fire.

   If one should think to purchase love,
      His hope would surely be forlorn;
  Though all his substance he would give,
      The suitor would be laughed to scorn;

8   'We have a sister, true,' they'd say,
      'So young her breasts are not yet grown.
  How can we help our sister, pray,
      Now you would take her for your own?

9   Shall we, if she is like a wall,
      Build silver turrets on her chest?
  Shall we, if she is like a gate,
      Fix cedar boards on for her breast?'

10  I was a wall, my breasts the towers
      That did defend the city gate,
  Till I became before him one
      That terms of peace did supplicate.

[8.5a]  The chorus echoes the scene of the marriage procession in
3.6ff. Just as then they wondered who it was coming up from the
desert, and it was the princess in her splendour, so now it is her again,
and she is leaning on the king's arm for all to see: 'Who is this coming
up from the desert, leaning on her beloved?' She is his favourite
consort, acknowledged in public.      [5bc]  The words suggest that
he was asleep in the royal arbour where David had once slept with
Bathsheba, but this is as usual only part of the truth. The couple
spent the night among the henna-blossom, and have slept together in
the morning (7.12f.); from which delights they are now returning to
the city. She 'awakened' him, that is, she roused him, not from sleep
only. 'There your mother conceived you, there she who bore you
conceived': *hibbᵉlâ*, 'writhed with', could be used of either conception or birth, but the birth is referred to in *yᵉlādatᵉkā*, and the
context requires conception—the word is used in this sense in Ps.
7.15. The repetition of both 'there' and 'she conceived' forcefully
suggest the sexual meaning: she roused him there where his mother
conceived him, i.e. in her womb—cf. 3.4, 'into my mother's house,
and into the chamber of her that conceived me'. He himself was
aroused 'under the apple tree'; perhaps a real tree is in mind, but the
male symbolism is there too from 2.3: see Introduction. Note that she
is suggesting herself subtly as the successor to Bathsheba's position
in other ways. He wore Bathsheba's crown at her wedding; they have
been united as she was when she conceived him; now the princess is
his favoured wife, and would be his Queen.

[6]  A man must never be parted from his seal. It was his
automatic signature (Jer. 32.10), with which important obligations
could be authorized. Judah wore his seal with a cord round his neck
(Gen. 38.18; cf. Prov. 3.3), whence her more poetic 'upon your heart'.
Pharaoh's was on his hand (Gen. 41.42), i.e. a signet ring; and this is
the meaning of her second phrase—*zᵉrû'â*, usually an arm in Heb.,
means a hand here; cf. 5.14, where 'his hands', i.e. his fingers, 'are
cylinders of gold'. She cannot be satisfied with any less close
association with him, 'for strong as death is love, and hard as Sheol is
jealousy'. Love is a passion inexorable, and she can know no peace
without his constant companionship; should he prefer another, the
pangs of jealousy would be an inescapable torment. I have transposed
v. 6c and v. 7a   [7a]  'Its flashes are flashes of fire, A flame of
Yahweh / A vehement flame. Many waters cannot quench love,
neither can the floods drown it.' She is not praising love; she is in awe

of its painful and indestructible power. The 'flashes' imply lightning, and the 'flame of Yahweh' is probably another way of speaking of the same thing, rather than a 'superlative' expression from a strong flame. The 'many' or 'mighty' waters are the ocean.

[7c, 8f]   But she also delights in it. The verses, which are a famous crux, make excellent sense if taken as direct speech following *yābûzû* (cf. 6.9f.—the otherwise standard Heb. *lē'môr*, 'saying', is absent from the Song): 'If a man will give all the substance of his house for love, with scorn will they scorn him' *and say* . . . The thread of thought is not as clear as usual: the poet means, Love is as strong as death, and you cannot buy it for money. The man offers his all, but the girl is only ten, and not mature enough to have any feelings for him.   [8]   'We have a little sister, but she has no breasts: what shall we do for our sister on the day that a proposal is made for her?' *bayyôm* = today, as at 3.11. The relatives of the (hypothetical) girl make merry at the expense of the wealthy but foolish suitor with a sequence of ironic questions.   [9]   is then part of this sequence emphasizing the absurdity. If she is (as flat as) a wall, would it help if they built two silver turrets on her (chest)? Heb. has *ṭîrat*, sing., a battlement, but the versions have correctly understood and pressed the image with a plural, turrets. If she is (as flat as) a gate, perhaps they could fix on a reinforcement of cedar boarding in a suitable position? In both cases the image arises from the girl being young, and so flat-chested, but both have the overtone of military defence, which is then exploited in the next verse. *delet*, normally a door, may be intended for the city-gate here, though the plural is used for this elsewhere: *ẓûr* II, to secure, enclose, suggests that the door is being reinforced against battering-rams. The obscurity of the 'little sister' section arises in part from the now familiar failure of the Song to distinguish physical from emotional response. But it is less trouble-some this time: ten-year-olds are emotionally as well as physically immature.   [10]   The princess takes up the image and applies it to herself. She was a wall and her breasts like the towers: i.e. she was a fortress of chastity. 'Then I became in his eyes as one bringing out peace.' When a city is surrendering, a delegation must come out offering, and suing for peace, like the burghers of Calais. *šālôm* means something close to 'terms of peace' in Deut. 20.10.

# Song 14

*The Queen*

*Chorus*

8.11 A vineyard Solomon did own;
    To tenant husbandmen he let
That vineyard in Baàl-Hamòn;
    A thousand shekels each he set

As rental for the fruit thereon—
*Princess*
12    Here is my vineyard that is mine:
Keep you your thousand, Solomon,
    You your two hundred, growers of wine.

[Enter King

*King*
13 O you who in the gardens dwell,
    Repeat the voice my comrades hear!
*Princess*
14 Leave them, my love; be a gazelle,
    Be on the perfumed hills a deer!

Two things make it probable that we should see Song 13 as ending at 8.10, and a short final Song (14) as beginning here. First the location and dramatis personae change. Song 13 opens with the royal couple coming up the desert road back into the city, while 14 is in the palace garden (v. 13). In the previous poem the king was addressed in 8.6, but he had become 'he' in v. 10. Now he is referred to as 'Solomon', and he enters and speaks in v. 13. We have had him enter in the course of a Song before (6.2), but never leave and enter. Secondly, the theme of Song 13 was the power of love as greater than money, and this closed with the development of the city–tower–gate–wall imagery in 8.10: now we have the different, vineyard image, which forms an inclusion with Song 1 (1.6), and completes the whole poem. So it seems best to attibute the opening verse to the Chorus. They have been the transition element in almost every Song, usually ending them, but sometimes, as at 8.5, opening the occasion. Verse 11 is a factual statement without emotion, and well suited to the Chorus.

[8.11] 'Solomon had a vineyard in Baal-Hamon. He let the vineyard to husbandmen: each was to bring for its fruit a thousand silver pieces.' There is a strong echo with Isaiah: 'My beloved had a vineyard in Horn of Fatness' (5.1), 'a thousand vines, worth a thousand shekels of silver' (7.23). Baal-Hamon, 'Ownalot', is a fictitious place, so far as we know. The king's wealth is fabulous: the land is so rich that the rent is 83% of the crop (v. 12). It is a real vineyard which is being spoken of, not the royal harem (Lys). We are to suppose that the king has gone to manage his property.

[12] 'My vineyard that is mine is before me'. In the previous Song the princess had made the appeal of a true lover, that she and the king should be inseparable as a man and his seal. Now we are to see whether her request is heard or not. The king, says the Chorus, had an enormous vineyard. He has two vineyards, she replies, and may choose between them: hers can yield him fruit of a different kind if he will—cf. on 1.6—and more delight than all his money.

[13] 'My comrades hear your voice: make me hear it.' Although he has been busy with his affairs off-stage, his nobles tell him that they can hear her voice; and that is the sum of his desire also. So he has chosen between his two vineyards: he really loves her, and has come to be with her. The gardens are both her actual haunts, and also the symbol of feminine delights (4.12, 15; 6.2).     [14]    Much the most common meaning of *bāraḥ* is 'flee', and this gives good

sense here: 'leave them'. So she has the final word. She makes him hear her voice indeed in a final invitation to love, that recalls the words of their courtship (2.17). She is the established queen: seen on the King's arm in public, and preferred by him to his business in the presence of his court. But the stress of the poet is not on her position as Queen, but as beloved: his princess is not a mean person with ulterior motives exploiting her attractions. She loves the king, and only lives to delight him.

## DISCUSSION

I hope that the foregoing translation and commentary may have established in the reader's judgment the two conclusions for which I have argued briefly in the Introduction. First, the Song is a single poem, and not a collection of unrelated lyrics: it moves through a sequence of fourteen scenes from the princess's arrival in Jerusalem to her acceptance as Solomon's beloved Queen. Second, the poet can be understood in practically every word as using his imagery in a precise and meaningful way; and this greatly increases the impact of the Song, and reveals its profoundly erotic character.

In this connection, it may be well to note here two formal points about the Song. The first concerns the function of the Chorus, which may be seen from a table of the individual Songs.

|      |                        |          | Chorus          |
| ---- | ---------------------- | -------- | --------------- |
| (1)  | The Arrival            | 1.1-8    | 1.7f, end       |
| (2)  | The Audience           | 1.9–2.7  | 2.7, end        |
| (3)  | The Courtship          | 2.8-17   |                 |
| (4)  | In the Night           | 3.1-5    | 3.5, end        |
| (5)  | The Procession         | 3.6-11   | 3.6-11, all     |
| (6)  | The Wedding            | 4.1-7    |                 |
| (7)  | The Consummation       | 4.8–5.1  | 5.1c, end       |
| (8)  | A Knock at the Door    | 5.2-9    | 5.8f, end       |
| (9)  | A Lover Lost and Found | 5.10–6.3 | 6.1             |
| (10) | The One and Only       | 6.4-12   |                 |
| (11) | The Dance              | 7.1-10   | 7.1, beginning  |
| (12) | A Night in the Country | 7.11–8.4 | 8.4, end        |
| (13) | Love's Demand          | 8.5-10   | 8.5a, beginning |
| (14) | The Queen              | 8.11-14  | 8.11, beginning |

I have marked under Chorus both the Chorus's actual participation and the princess's references to them, and it can be seen how often one or other of these devices is used to separate the Songs from one another—six times at the end, three times at the beginning, once (6.1) after the lyric and before the dialogue, and once to speak the whole Song (Song 5). But there is nothing automatic about it: when it does not seem suitable to include them, because the couple are alone or for some other reason, they are left out. The other feature, which I take to be intentional, is that there are fourteen Songs, two sevens: the poem divides in two neatly at 5.1, with the Consummation at the climax of the first seven.

But although we may now claim, with all due tentativeness, to have understood the Song, at least in outline, there remains a whole series of questions about its setting in Israelite life; and unless we can think of plausible answers to these, our understanding will remain on a very superficial level. When was the Song written? Was its author intending merely to write an erotic idyll, or does some more subtle purpose underlie it? Does it have any theological thrust, and if not, how did it come to be included in the Bible? If it was included in Scripture for what it seems to be, how is it that we find no trace of the erotic interpretation in the (many) rabbinic comments on it, but rather a solid tradition of allegorization? If it is generally true that worship sanctified the biblical material—law, narrative, psalms, prophecies, everything—over a period of generations before they were canonized in the Bible, can we think of any way in which the Song might have had its roots in worship? It is such problems that we have not yet attempted to answer.

### The Date

There are two periods which are likely candidates for the Song's composition. Solomon was an honoured figure in Judah during his long reign in the tenth century, and after; but with the rise of the Deuteronomic tradition his reputation suffered an eclipse, due to his love of money, horses and women, and especially to his tolerance of the heathen worship of the last. However, after settling down on their return from Exile, people remembered his wisdom and greatness with more affection; and it is from this period—down to the early years of the Christian era—that books with his name were either written or edited. Some of these have been included in the Bible, like the Proverbs (of Solomon, 1.1), or Ecclesiastes (the Preacher, the son of David, 1.1); others have not, like the Wisdom of Solomon, or the Psalms or Odes of Solomon.

It is often thought[47] that we could honour the Solomonic tradition. Solomon had a sophisticated court, and singing men and women were already part of it in his father's time (2 Sam. 19.35). Love poetry not dissimilar from the Song in its ideas and images is known from contemporary Egypt; and Egypt was influential in Solomon's day. He is said to have composed a thousand and five songs (1 Kgs 4.32) himself. Even though Proverbs in its present form is post-exilic, it embodies sayings, and probably collections of sayings, that go back to Solomon's time;[48] and this was a period when the human was valued in its own right. Thus we should have an excellent setting for the Song. It will have begun as royal entertainment, singing of the king and his love; it will have been preserved for its beauty (and eroticism). Its venerability will have ensured its ultimate inclusion in Scripture, although some doubted (m. Yad. 3.5); and the embarrassment was saved by the allegorical interpretation.

We may certainly allow that a tradition of love-songs was preserved in court circles from early times, and that the mode was remembered, and perhaps some examples; but the theory has an embarrassing gap, in that there was no royal court after 586, and it is not too likely that the Song was included in Scripture after two centuries and more of disuse. There are no Egyptian pieces which approach the Song in length or complexity; and the relevance of the Egyptian parallels adduced by Gerleman and others is not always obvious. Although Proverbs might provide a parallel, as a book whose core goes back to early times, in its present form it is certainly post-exilic, and indeed probably contains an echo of the Song itself (23.31); and the remaining Solomon books, Ecclesiastes, Wisdom, the Psalms and the Odes, were all written *de novo* in the late period. It seems curious, too, to accept a venerable erotic poem into the canon, and then to foist an allegorical interpretation on to it. It was certainly known to be erotic in the late period: Ecclesiastes contains a number of acid parodies of its wording[49]—'the crackling of *thorns* under a *pot*' is a play on 'the Song of Songs'—and Aqiba forbad its chanting in public houses (t. Sanh. 12.10).

A late date, in the fourth/third centuries, is made probable by the language. The Song may contain a number of Persian words,[50] but one that is certain is *pardēṣ* (4.13), an orchard or park. Persia did not become a power in the Levant till the middle of the sixth century, four hundred years after Solomon. *pardēṣ* is used in two other texts from the Persian period or later, Neh. 2.8 and Eccl. 2.5; the Greek form, *paradeisos,* is used by the fourth-century author Xenophon. It would be natural for some Persian words to be taken into Hebrew during the two centuries that Israel was in the Persian Empire, down to 332. But the Song also contains many words which are not found elsewhere in the Bible, but which we find in Aramaic, like *s$^e$tāw,* winter, or in post-biblical Hebrew, like *mēṣab,* a couch. It could be, of course, that Solomon employed foreign Aramaic-speaking singers, and that the rabbis took words over from the Song; but the balance of probability must incline towards a fourth-century date, when Aramaic was coming to be quite generally spoken. An especially striking instance is the common use (32 times) of the particle *š$^e$,* that, for the classical Hebrew *'$^a$šer. š$^e$* is normal in late Hebrew, and comes 139 times in the Bible, of which 68 are in Ecclesiastes (3rd/2nd cent.), and a number in some of the later psalms in Book V. It is true that it does also occur in the early text, the Song of Deborah (12th cent.), Jg. 5.7, so that the argument is not conclusive; but nonetheless it remains weighty. Some further considerations to the same end are given by Landy, p. 18.

### A Doctrine Implied

A fourth- or third-century date is suggestive of a theological theme for the Song. At first sight we are inclined to see the poem as an erotic idyll of ideal love: the story of a girl of perfect beauty which captured the heart of a king. 'My love is perfect to each sense. There is no blemish-spot in her.' With so many praises of the heroine's perfections, it is easy to forget that, to normal Israelite thinking, there is in fact one serious imperfection: she is 'black' (1.5). The fact is freely confessed by the similes following:-

> 'Black am I but lovely, O daughters of Jerusalem,
> As the tents of Kedar, as the curtains of Solomon.'

Bedouin tents are certainly very dark, and Solomon's curtains are probably to be taken in the same sense. The poet is well aware of the Israelite feeling towards very dark women: 'Stare not at me, though darkened I be, that the sun has beheld me' (1.6). He proceeds to excuse her being so dark: it was not her fault, it was her horrid brothers who forced her to work in the sun. By *nature* she would have been light. The fact of her 'blackness' is thus established and apologized for in the opening verses.

There is no further reference to her dark skin; but there are, if I have interpreted them correctly, a series of references to her curly hair. In 4.1 and 6.5 the king compares her hair to a flock of goats, and the image implies a crowd of units, which would correspond to curls rather than to sleek locks or plaits. In 7.5 her head is like Carmel, and her hair is as purple; 'the king is bound in its troughs'. The purple sounds very black, and both the binding and the 'watertroughs' suggest rings. Thus her 'black' features are not forgotten, and are likely to be in mind also at 7.5, 'Your neck is like a tower of ivory', by contrast. Indeed, her dark skin and fuzzy hair stand in clear contrast with her loved one's 'shining, ruddy' complexion and smooth, black hair, like a raven (5.10f.), which are the Israelite ideal. She much admires his 'golden' head, hands and feet.

She is not a negress, but comes from Arabia, and this cannot be an accident. She is 'daughter of Nadiv' (7.2), and speaks of Nadiv as 'my people' (6.12). There can be little doubt that an Arabian home has been suggested for her by the story of the Queen of Sheba; but it is not likely that she is supposed to be the Queen of Sheba, partly because the 1 Kgs 10 story makes it plain that the Queen returned to her home after the visit, and partly because, if it were intended, Sheba and not Nadiv would be given as her people. Solomon is not mentioned in the history as having a particular queen (no doubt because he had too many), so our author could choose where his heroine should come from: and he has chosen a land of unrelenting sunlight, whose natives are markedly darker than Israelites with their long cool winter. He tells us that the sun darkens them (1.6): so her darkness is a deliberately chosen and recurrent feature that runs counter to the otherwise steady emphasis on her perfection. There must be some reason for this.

Why should the author have deliberately introduced this negative element into his heroine? I would suggest that the Song belongs in the context of the fourth-century Jewish controversy on intermarriage with foreign women. Nehemiah, and later Ezra, had found the little Jerusalem community in process of assimilation to the neighbouring countries. Foreign women could not be expected to keep Israelite worship pure, and their children did not even speak Hebrew: both leaders instituted policies of compulsory divorce from foreign wives. But such a firm line can never be universally popular, nor can nature be expelled with a fork; and we have evidence of a persevering liberal movement within Judaism which welcomed foreign marriages. Ruth is a good instance of this liberalism. Ruth is a Moabitess, but a girl of exemplary character, devoted to her tedious mother-in-law, and determined to raise up seed to her husband; and she was received into the Israelite community, married the distinguished Boaz, and ultimately became the ancestress of King David himself. The tale is told with enormous skill. Our sympathies are enlisted from the beginning. The marriages of Naomi's sons with Moabite girls took place only because of the dreadful famine in Israel. Moabites are Israel's closest and best neighbours, related by blood as children of Lot; and David sent his parents to Moab during the troubles with Saul. Thus the thin end of the wedge is firmly driven in: intermarriage can be marvellously and manifestly blessed by God.

The same battle is being fought centuries later in the tract, Joseph and Aseneth[51]. Joseph had spent his young adulthood in Egypt, and the Genesis story credits him with marrying Aseneth, daughter of the Egyptian high priest, as one of the highest aristocrats on the contemporary market. Later Biblical writers regarded marriage with Egyptians as a sign of apostasy: Hagar married Ishmael to an Egyptian girl, and even Moses was accused of marrying an Egyptian. But Joseph's marriage is there in the Bible, and the author of Joseph and Aseneth turns it to account. Aseneth becomes a pattern proselyte, devoted to Jewish ways, a paragon of virtue and piety. So (runs the unpressed conclusion) marriage with an Egyptian woman can be marvellous too: even the patriarch Joseph...

The liberals had a long fight on their hands: not just Nehemiah and Ezra, but the whole D-tradition was against them. So it would not be surprising if they cast around the scriptural tradition for some other noted Israelite who had married abroad with success. Who then would leap to mind more quickly than Solomon, whose star, thanks to the current devotion to 'wisdom', was now in the ascendant? Solomon was famous for the number of his foreign wives; the only unfortunate aspect of Solomon was that he was also famous for being corrupted by them. So the author wisely eschews any attempt to paint his princess as a pious convert to Judaism. Solomon was also famous for his songs, and he composes a love-song (perhaps from some traditional model) in which he enlists the sympathy of the listener for the dark, foreign bride with just as much skill as did the author of Ruth. His appeal depends upon a more profound human emotion than the fear of miscegenation—romantic, sexual love. His heroine never mentions religion; but she loved Solomon with all her heart, and with her beauty and affection she made him happy. Solomon had the world to choose from, and he came to love this dark girl with her fuzzy hair the best of all his harem, better than all the Jewish girls, the 'daughters of Jerusalem', who form so pliable a chorus, better even than the celebrated beauty, Abishag. So (subtly unexpressed) runs the corollary once more, Israelites can marry foreigners today, can they not, and be equally happy? And not just Moabites either, whom you cannot tell from an Israelite by looking, but girls from far-off places like Nadiv in Arabia, where the complexion and hair-growth is so distinctive. Neither Ruth nor Joseph and Aseneth press their conclusions into words: their art is to win their hearers' sympathy for their heroines, and then to let them draw their own conclusion. The Song is the same.

We find a small but significant hint that this interpretation is correct from a repeated linguistic feature of the poem. Down to 4.7, the marriage laudation, the king addresses the princess regularly as *ra'yātî*, my companion; she is, in addition, once 'my dove' (2.14). After the marriage ceremony, he calls her *kallâ*, bride, in each of the five following verses (4.8-12), which is understandable; but in three of these he says *'ᵃhôtî kallâ*, my sister-bride, and the same phrase comes at the actual moment of union, 5.1. She is 'my sister' along with other endearments again when he knocks on the door at 5.2. This expression, which has caused so much puzzlement, seems to be satisfactorily explained if the writer's aim is to legitimate foreign marriages. As soon as the dark princess was taken to Solomon's bed, she became a naturalized Israelite, as much his sister as any Jewish woman. The emphasis would have perhaps surprised the royal lover in history: but it is not history that I am expounding. The poet makes him call her his sister five times in ten verses, and the repetition and the singularity of the expression alike stress its significance.

It seems plausible, therefore, to conclude that the Song is a fourth-century liberal tract, whose purpose is to win acceptance for foreign marriages; for unless there is such an intention, it is difficult to explain the recurring emphasis on its heroine's darkness, curly hair, and Arabian extraction, which alone detract from her oft-sung perfections. This is part of a theological battle in contemporary society: the Song is the most ambitiously anti-racialist document in the Bible. The cataclysm of 586 brought forth a series of defenders of the laager: the D-historian, Ezra and Nehemiah all thought God's will was the purity of the Jewish race. But a more generous response was persistent, and in the end victorious: Third Isaiah, Malachi, Jonah, Ruth and the Song all pleaded the acceptability of Gentiles, especially Gentile women, in Israel, under suitable specifications. The liberals won only because they were able to produce writings of skill and power which could be recited frequently, and so become part of the corpus of received tradition, and ultimately of the canon. The Song is the most strikingly anti-racialist of the five, because it has accepted the democratic principle completely. Elsewhere the Jews are the privileged people, who will welcome Gentiles to their God's temple, or carry the word of repentance to them. In the Song there are no privileges. All the women compete on a par for Solomon's love, and our princess carries the day by her beauty, her affection and her persistence. The unspoken, and unintended, implication is that Jews and Gentiles are equal in the sight of God. Such theological insights do not receive explicit expression before the Epistle to the Ephesians.

The discovery of what seems to be a theological drive in a book where God's name is never mentioned resolves our major difficulty. We can understand, if this is so, how the Song came to be included in scripture. It was part of the liberal party's manifesto, and it would have the liberals behind it, wanting to have it recited, and respecting it as an inspired word from God. All theories that deny a theological message to the Song fail at this hurdle. It is useless to claim that the Song proves Israel's acceptance of secular, sexual love as a gift from God: there is no hint of anything so modern in the text. Nor can we plausibly say that the very secularity is theological, because it constitutes a denial of the sexual mythology in other religions. For a book to be included in the canon it must be accepted by a large section of the community as conveying a word of God. The Song has such a message: 'God gave love as the basis for marriage, not birth or colour. You may marry whom you will.' I will not say that its cause was not helped forward by the erroneous belief that it was written by Solomon; or that its great beauty and delicacy did not commend it; or that its eroticism did not tell in its favour; or ultimately a misguided mystical and allegorical exegesis. But manufacturers of motor-cars know that you must have a genuine product to sell as well as a naked girl on the bonnet; and the primary reason for the Song's success was not its supposed authorship, or its poetry, or its erotic appeal, but its implied theology.

## Love and Sex

Such high claims may perhaps strike the reader as exaggerated and unreal. Surely, he may feel, the very detail of the foregoing translation and exegesis belies them. They reveal the Song, if we are to be forthright, as nothing else than a piece of high-class pornography; and the present expositor as the last of a long line of biblical students who have deceived themselves by attributing to it a spiritual meaning, under a motivation all too obvious. The princess is portrayed from the first verse as a virtual nymphomaniac, lusting to be kissed on the mouth by a man she has never met (1.2), overwhelmed with passion from the moment she meets him (1.12), proceeding in a manner that can only be called abandoned (2.4-6). There is much talk of love in the poem, but the author does not distinguish love from sex: 'his standard on me is love' (2.4) means that the king is excited by her; ''tis love such gracefulnesses bring' (7.7) is what he says, but what they actually bring is desire (7.8f.). The repeated praises of her say nothing whatever of her character or her mind; they are praises of her body, and the technique of moving from top to toe, or vice versa, and including the sexual organs, has the effect, and the motive, of titillation. Titillation is the key-note: the whole elaborate structure of similes and metaphors enables author and hearer to feast their lusts, and the more indirect and the more delicate the comparison, the more suggestive and arousing the effect. The virtuous reader must emerge from such a study feeling soiled and disgusted. It would seem that there is no innocent feature of the glad Maytime among God's plants and fruits and animals, or the works of man, but may be turned to account by a prurient imagination. The character of the king confirms this unhappy picture: he is nothing but a sexual performer, never sleeping but constantly making the round of his seraglio (3.1ff.; 5.2ff.); returning to his bride with desire unexhausted, twice (3.4; 6.3); able at once to renew the battle (6.12); valued for nothing but his good looks and his potency (5.14). The sexual extravagances of 6.12, 7.10 and 8.2 are better passed over in silence.

We cannot but allow that there is some justice to our virtuous reader's objection; but it is important to see that it is not the whole truth. The princess desires the king from the beginning; but this is not reprehensible in a bride, and there is nothing crude about their courtship and love-making—rather their delicacy makes the poem a classic of love-poetry. What cannot be allowed is the imputation that sex and not love is the writer's concern. The beautiful courtship song in 2.8-17 speaks to the reader of romantic love; the princess loves the king, and goes after him at some considerable risk in 3.1f., and at the price of pain and humiliation in 5.7; her praise of him in 5.10-16, and her confession that he is making love to his other women in 6.2f., achieve a high level of pathos; 6.3, by contrast, 'I am my beloved's . . . ' speaks of love's triumph, and the famous lines, 'For love is strong as death . . . ' (8.6f.) can stand alongside love-poetry in any language. The Song is an erotic poem, but it is about love and not sex. The male is praised as well as the female (5.10-16). Nor should we be deceived by the physical emphasis. It is not in dispute that David loved Jonathan, but all he mentions in his famous lament is Jonathan's looks, his strength and his fleetness of foot. We must judge ancient literature by ancient norms. Ruth and Job and Dan. 2–7 use other contemporary modes to enlist their hearers' sympathy for a cause held to be, at the profoundest level, religious; and the Song uses the mode of the erotic love-poem. The author has produced an artistic masterpiece, and Herder was right to say that disgust with it is prudery.[52]

### A Setting in Israelite Life

We may claim then to have some understanding both of the plot and imagery of the Song, and of its driving message. But how are we to imagine such a work as finding its way into circulation? At first sight, the poem seems to give us little means of answering such a question. The form of the poem, with its unbroken dialogue, is unparalleled in the OT. It is closest to the Book of Job, but without the latter's prologue and epilogue; but we do not know how Job came to gain its place in the canon, still less its place in Jewish religious life. Again, we have found the Song to have fourteen sub-songs, and this sounds a significant feature; but it is hard to draw any dependable conclusion from it. Commentators often call the Song a tract; but there is something radically unsatisfying about the associations of 'tract', a word that explains nothing, and is redolent of anachronisms—Dr Pusey, and printing presses, and eager people on street corners. Other parts of scripture matured in the Jewish community's worship, and we should be more comfortable if we could suggest a concrete setting for the Song in Israelite worship from the beginning. It will then be less of a problem to understand how it came to be included in the Bible. I close therefore with a final suggestion of a tentative kind.

In *The Evangelists' Calendar*[53] I made a short study of some of the books in the Writings, and noted a striking feature common to Ruth, Job and the Aramaic chapters of Daniel (2–7). They all seemed to draw their inspiration from the same area of the Law, Gen. 36–41. Ruth is like Tamar in Gen. 38. Both are foreign women married to Israelites whose husbands die without issue; both aspire to raise up seed to their dead husbands through Levirate marriages, and both require determination and feminine guile to achieve their object. Indeed, the book of Ruth closes with the women saying to the heroine, 'Let thy house be like the house of Perez, whom Tamar bare unto Judah'. Job is Jobab of Gen. 36.33f.—or was believed so to be both by the LXX (in the appendix to the book), and by Pseudo-Philo, but with different wives and children.[54] Uz, Eliphaz, Teman, Bilhan (= Bildad) and Zepho (= Zophar) are all mentioned in this chapter. Daniel repeatedly stands before kings and interprets their dreams and visions, and gains promotion thereby, just like Joseph in Gen. 41; innocent like Joseph, he was also the victim of a conspiracy and thrown into a pit (Gen. 37), but God saved his life and brought him to power. For further details I must refer the reader to the discussion, pp. 184–99.

The question then arises why so many stories should seem to be meditations on the same area of the Bible, and I made the following proposal. Gen. 37–40 is read in synagogues to this day as the ninth *sidra* (law-reading) of the year's cycle of fifty-four. At the time, the cycle began from the first month, Nisan, our April,[55] so Gen. 37–40 would have been read on the ninth sabbath, Gen. 41ff. on the tenth; and these two sabbaths would normally fall to either side of the feast of Pentecost, which is on the 65th day of the year (6th Sivan, the third month). So perhaps Pentecost, the feast of the giving of the Law, was observed as an opportunity for such meditations as Ruth, Job and Daniel: and in fact Ruth is still read in synagogues at Pentecost to this day. In favour of such a suggestion was the fact that other passages, from the prophetic books, were also drawn on in the same way, 1 Sam. 1–4, Hos. 13 and Isa. 13; and all these passages fall about the same distance through their respective corpus. Pentecost is about a fifth of the way through the year; Gen. 37 is about a fifth of the way through the 187 chapters of the Law; Isa. 13 is about a fifth of the way through the 66 chapters of Isaiah, and Hos. 13 about a fifth of the way through the 67 chapters of the Twelve Minor Prophets, which the Jews count as a single unit. 1 Samuel begins nearly a third of the way through the History books, but special considerations apply.[56]

Now sauce for the goose should be sauce for the gander. If Ruth and Job and Dan. 2–7 came into existence in the context of Pentecostal worship, under the inspiration of Gen. 37–41, Hos. 13 and 1 Sam. 1–3, we might look at the same scriptures to see if they could have acted as material for the inspiration of the Song.

One point will immediately have struck the reader. We have noticed repeatedly in commenting on the text, that although the Song has traditionally been used in Jewish worship at Passover (since the seventh century of our era), the time described in the poem is Maytime, or even early June; and that is the season of Pentecost. Henna (1.14) blossoms in June, and it is then that the lily flowers (2.2) and the apples are formed (2.3, 5), and the young animals frolic, the fawns bounding over the hills (2.9), and the fox-cubs (2.15). The rain is past by early May (2.11), and there are flowers and birdsong from March (2.12); the turtledove is to be heard from May, being a summer migrant (2.12), and in May and June the green figs turn red, and the vines are in fragrant flower (2.13). Sheep-shearing (4.2) is at Pentecost-tide, and the ewes may be seen with their lambs through the spring; nature's scents are then at their richest (4.16), with the pomegranate in flower (6.11) and the mandrake fruiting (7.13). Pentecost too is wheat-harvest (7.2). Of course, some things in the poem do not coincide: wine and pomegranate fruits, dates and vine-clusters. But the overwhelming mass of the imagery belongs in the late spring, at Pentecost-time, and encourages us to think that the poem was composed for use then.

When we come to look for possible inspiration for the imagery from particular passages, we must exercise considerable caution; for some images—vine, sheep, etc.—may be found in many places, and we need to read widely to see if there are enough images in any one section to be significant. What we are looking for is rarer words, and concentrations; and the greater part of any correspondence should be in Hebrew (underlined in what follows).

There is no significant concentration of images in the Law outside Genesis, nor anything striking before Gen. 30. There Leah says *'Daughters will call* me *blessed'* (30.13); Cant. 6.9, 'Daughters saw and called her blessed'. In the days of the wheat-harvest Reuben found *mandrakes* in the *field* (30.14): Cant. 7.12ff., 'Let us go forth into the field . . . The mandrakes give forth fragrance'. Jacob bred his flocks by the *watering-troughs* (30.38, 41), which the king likens to his bride's curls (7.5); and he brought sheep and *goats from Gilead* (31.46ff.) to *Mahanaim* (32.2), again recalling our heroine's hair 'like a flock of goats appearing from Mount Gilead' (4.1f.; 6.5), and perhaps the dance of Mahanaim (7.1).

There is no clear lead again before Gen. 37. Joseph dreams of the sun and the moon and the eleven stars (Gen. 37.9), and I have suggested above the possibility of this text standing behind Cant. 6.10, 'fair as the moon, bright as the sun, awesome as the bannered ones'. At Gen. 37.16 Joseph says of his brothers, '*Tell me*, pray, where are they *pasturing*?': cf. Cant. 1.7, 'Tell me, you whom my soul loves, where do you pasture?' Later in the chapter Joseph is rescued from the pit by a caravan of Ishmaelite traders from Gilead bearing gum, balm and myrrh (v. 25); these could be related to the myrrh and frankincense and all the fragrant powders of the merchant (Cant. 3.6), but the Hebrew words are different. The Tamar story gives more confidence. Judah goes down to Timnah at the time of sheep-shearing (Gen. 38.12): cf. Cant. 4.2, 'Your teeth are like a flock of shorn ewes'. Tamar has disguised herself as a whore, and accepts as pledge of payment his *seal* and cord from around his neck (v. 18): cf. 8.6, 'Make me as the seal upon your heart'. He undertakes to pay her a *kid* of the *goats* (v. 17): cf. 1.8, 'Feed your kids', and 4.1, 6.5, 'Like streaming goats your curly hair'. In the course of time she bears *twins* (v. 27, perhaps we should compare 4.2, 'All of them have borne twins'), and the hand of Zerah is bound with a *scarlet* thread: cf. 4.3, 'Your lips are like a scarlet cord'. More generally Tamar means a palm-tree, and the dance-song concludes with the image of the palm-tree: 'You are tall as a *tāmār* . . . I'll clamber up the *tāmār*' (7.8f.). We may think also of Tamar as the prime biblical precedent for a woman offering herself honourably in sex, and so as a natural type of the princess; and perhaps also by association of Absalom's *beautiful sister* Tamar (2 Sam. 13.1), whose half-brother Amnon *loved* her and slept with her. The Tamar story is likely to underlie the Song because (i) the general similarity makes the detailed similarities plausible: (ii) it contains the only reference in the Bible to a seal worn round the neck, apart from Cant. 8.6, and scarlet threads are not common either; and (iii) even where the images are relatively common, they are concentrated, both in Gen. 38 on the one side and in Cant. 4.1ff. on the other.

When we return to Joseph, our confidence is less strong. The butler tells Joseph his dream of the vine: 'And on the *vine* there were three branches; as soon as it *budded*, its *blossoms* shot forth, and the *clusters* ripened into grapes' (Gen. 40.10). Perhaps we should compare Cant. 2.13, 6.11, etc., but the language is common. In 41.42 *Pharaoh* gives Joseph the signet-ring from his hand, and makes him ride in the second *chariot*. We may think of Cant. 8.6 again, 'as the seal of your hand', a very rare feature in the Bible, though the Hebrew differs; and of 1.9, the chariots of Pharaoh. The rest of Genesis is even more undependable.

A second passage which I mentioned as influential (on Dan. 7 especially) was Hos. 13, and the leaping ('*āšûr, tāšûrî*) of the lion and the *leopard* in 4.8/Hos. 13.7 encourages us to look at the passage seriously. In 14.4–7 Hosea writes: 'I will heal their faithlessness; I will *love* them freely, for my anger has turned from them. I will be as the *dew* to Israel; he shall *bud as the lily*, he shall strike root as *Lebanon*; his shoots shall spread out; his beauty shall be like the olive, and his *fragrance like Lebanon*. They shall return and *dwell beneath his shadow*, they shall grow grain; they shall *bud* as *the vine*, their fragrance shall be like the *wine* of *Lebanon*.' Here, as in Gen. 38, the echoes ring thickly with the song. 'My head is wet with dew' (5.2); 'as a lily among thorns' (2.2); 'to see whether the vines have budded' (6.11); 'his appearance is as Lebanon' (5.15); 'the fragrance of your garments is as the fragrance of Lebanon' (4.11): 'I delight in its shadow and sit down' (*bᵉṣillô yšb*, 2.3, as in Hos. 14.7).

As with the Tamar story, here are several considerations which make it likely that our poet has drawn inspiration from the prophecy. (i) The whole general theme of the book of Hosea is marital love, and the supreme exemplar proposed is Yahweh's own love for Israel his bride. Hence there is a rather plausible motive to hand for the Song to take up Hos. 14: married love was already established as a Pentecostal theme. (ii) Later Jewish exegesis was then free simply to reverse the process, and to interpret the Song as a poem about the love of Yahweh for Israel. It is surely unlikely that so universal an interpretative tradition should be utterly wrong; and here is the means to understand its origin. The Song was a meditation on Yahweh's love for Israel in Hos. 14, transferred to the human level; and all the rabbis and their predecessors have done is to read it as a meditation on Yahweh's love for Israel in Hosea. (iii) We may note again the concentration of images: both in four verses of Hosea, and especially in the consummation song in Cant. 4.9–5.1, 'Come with me from Lebanon . . . leap . . . from the dens of lions, from the mountains of leopards . . . How much better is your love than wine . . . the fragrance of your garments is like the fragance of Lebanon . . . a garden fountain (Hos. 13.15), and flowing streams from Lebanon'.

Hosea is the first book of the twelve Minor Prophets, and the second is Joel. Since we have found so strong an echo of the Song in the last chapter of Hosea, we should glance at Joel 1; where it is said, 'The *vine* withers, the *fig tree* languishes. *Pomegranate*, palm and apple, all the trees of the field are withered' (v. 11). It is very striking to find five of the most frequent images of the Song there in a single verse. It might be replied that the Song is drawing on the salient features of nature, and that includes the five best known fruit-trees; and not surprisingly, these all feel the effect of Joel's drought at the same time. We must, for lack of further evidence, leave this point open; but it seems very likely that the Song has drawn inspiration at least from Hos. 14, which must (on my hypothesis) have been read at or about Pentecost each year.

Naturally there are other scriptural associations behind the Song. Gold and cedar and spices and a princess from Arabia (Sheba) all come in 1 Kgs 10. Isa. 5 opens, 'Let me sing of *my beloved a song of my beloved* touching his vineyard. *My beloved had a vineyard* on a very fertile hill . . . '; Isa. 7.23 prophesies disaster for 'every place where there were a thousand vines at *a thousand silver shekels*'. The echo with Cant. 8.11 is clear, 'Solomon had a vineyard at Baal-hamon . . . each one was to bring for its fruit a thousand silver shekels'; and there is the ubiquitous 'my beloved'. But neither chapter seems to be further exploited. Isa. 13 is not a clear source either. It contains an ensign (v. 2), the stars of heaven and their constellations, the sun and the moon (v. 10), *fine gold* (*paz*) and *gold* (*ketem*, v. 12, cf. Cant. 5.11, 'His head is *ketem paz*), men fleeing like a *roe* (v. 14), and *shepherds making* (their flocks) *lie down* (v. 20). There is some rarity among these expressions, however. *Ketem* and *paz* are found together in only Isa. 13.12, Cant. 5.11 and Prov. 8.19; and *hirbiṣ*, to make to lie down, without an expressed object, occurs only at Isa. 13.20 and Cant. 1.7.

We should not leave the Pentecostal proposal without a brief consideration of the psalms in use at the festival; of which 1, 19 and 119 are meditations on the Law, and were probably composed or adapted in early times for use at the festival. Again we have a combination of images including the rare word *bārāḥ*, shining or pure, in Ps. 19: 'The commandment of the LORD is *shining* . . . More *to be desired* are they than gold, even much *fine gold*; Sweeter also than *honey* and drippings of the honeycomb' (vv. 4–6): so we have a strong case for thinking that Ps. 19 lies behind Cant. 6.9f., 'Shining to her that bore her . . . shining as the sun'—indeed the word for 'sun', *ḥammâ*, also comes of the sun's heat in Ps. 19.6 'nothing is hidden from its *ḥammâ*'. It has probably also influenced 5.16, 'His palate is most sweet, and he is altogether desirable'. Once the psalm is established as an influence, we also have 4.11, 'Your lips drip nectar, my bride; Honey and milk are under your tongue'. We find a similar sentiment in the otherwise barren Ps. 119, 'How sweet are thy words to *my palate*, sweeter than honey to my mouth' (v. 103).

It seems then that it is possible to resolve the major problems connected with the Song. It is a single poem, a Song of fourteen songs, that brings the princess from her arrival at Solomon's court to an established position as his Queen-Consort. Its imagery is carefully thought out, and for the most part strongly erotic. It stems from the late biblical period, probably the third century. It has a theological message of an anti-particularist kind: God wills that his people may marry whom they will, as wise King Solomon did of old. It shares this message with other late Biblical books like Ruth; and in part Job, which has also a non-Israelite from the desert for hero. Like the Song, such books saw the light through the opportunity given at Pentecost for the exposition of the traditional themes of the feast. Our author drew to some extent on the details of Gen. 30–31 from preceding weeks, but his main inspiration was the Tamar story in Gen. 38 and the final chapter of Hosea; Isaiah (5, 7, 13) and Ps. 19 and perhaps Joel 1 also contributed. The Song won its way to favour and into the Canon by virtue of its message, its beauty, its eroticism and its false ascription. But objection was reasonably made that it was conducive to lust, and R. Aqiba forbad its use in taverns (t. Sanh. 12.10). This fear led to a solid interpretative tradition that ignored its original meaning, and construed every phrase as an allegory of God's love for Israel, and Israel's response. The path to such an interpretation was to hand in the very scriptures on which the Song had leaned for inspiration: in the psalm which said that what was sweet to the palate was not kisses but the Law, and in the prophecy which saw the lily and the budding vine and wine and the fragrance of Lebanon as symbolizing the love not of Solomon but of Yahweh.

# NOTES

1. *The Servant of the Lord, and Other Essays in the Old Testament* (London, 1952), pp. 189-234.

2. *'Le Plus Beau Chant' de la Création* (Lectio Divina, 51; Paris, 1968), pp. 31-55.

3. The most recent of these is A. Robert's *Le Cantique des Cantiques*, completed by R. Tournay with A. Feuillet (Paris, 1963); allowance is made for a human love-poem, but the stress is on the divine relation with Israel subtending it.

4. E.g. W.J. Ouweneel, *Das Lied der Lieder* (Wuppertal, 1976).

5. *Song of Songs* (Anchor Bible; New York, 1977). Lys's book is a subtle attempt to make something of all the various approaches: he sees the Tammuz-Ishtar myths as a kind of back-drop to a love-poem which is a meditation on Gen. 2.

6. *Ruth. Das Hohelied* (BKAT, 18; Neukirchen-Vluyn, 1965). Gerleman's commentary is a mine of reliable information in a reasonable compass; I am much indebted to it, although I rarely concur in its conclusions.

7. *The Song of Songs and Lamentations* (New York, 1974, revised from 1954); it contains a number of valuable suggestions which I have appropriated with gratitude.

8. *Paradoxes of Paradise* (Sheffield, 1983). The opening chapter contains a critique of much current writing on the Song, often acute. The remainder is sympathetic to Lys with a vision of Paradise behind the text; but Landy does not limit himself to the poet's intentions (p. 183).

9. Lys devotes considerable space to a running demolition of Robert–Tournay and other allegorists, and of T.J. Meek's myth-liturgy view from *The Interpreter's Bible* (New York/Nashville, 1956). But his own nuanced approach seems interesting rather than convincing—e.g. his alignment of Solomon (root *šlm*, fullness) and the black girl (*šḥrh*) with the Ugaritic divinities Shahar (*šḥr*) and Shalim (*šlym*), Dusk and Dawn, p. 70.

10. Rowley, pp. 202-206, Gerleman, pp. 50f., Gordis, pp. 10ff. The best representative of the dramatic view is F. Delitzsch, *Hoheslied und Koheleth* (Leipzig, 1875), with six pairs of scenes and two characters, Solomon and a country-girl.

11. Gerleman, p. 174. Gerleman relates the doves to Egyptian statues.

12. John Healey, 'The Song of Songs', in J.H. Eaton, ed. *Readings in Biblical Hebrew II* (Birmingham, 1978), pp. 120-33, a fine introduction to the Song: the remark cited is on p. 131. J.C. Exum's interesting article, 'A literary and structural analysis of the Song of Songs', is in *ZAW* (1973), pp. 47-79.

13. Robert, p. 55.

14. OED gives 'black port-wine, 1859'; cf. Latin *niger* = swarthy, Vergil,

*Eclogue* 2.16, and many languages. The excuse about the brothers implies that she is dark, not black.

15.  *Nat. Hist.* 12.14.30, §52.

16.  The Queen of Sheba is not very suitable as according to 1 Kgs 10.13 she went home after the visit; nor could there be any obvious reason for not giving the name. The rabbinic tradition does not think of the princess as the Queen of Sheba.

17.  C.M. Doughty, *Travels in Arabia Deserta* (London, 1926), pp. 226-41.

18.  Columella, *De Re Rustica*, 5.3, describes the rows as being from five to nine feet apart.

19.  Doughty, p. 224.

20.  G. Dalman, *Arbeit und Sitte in Palästina* (Gütersloh, 1928-), II, p. 301.

21.  *Die Flora der Juden*, I-III (Vienna, Leipzig, 1924-28).

22.  *Plants of the Bible* (Cambridge, 1982).

23.  Nearly an inch of rain falls at Safad in Galilee in an average May, but elsewhere the rain is nearly over by the end of April—0.1 in. is the average in May in Jerusalem (H.G. May [ed.], *Oxford Bible Atlas* [2nd edn; Oxford, 1974], p. 50).

24.  Some figs in Palestine develop from the green fruit-buds which are already formed over the winter. It is 'not the season of figs' at Passover (Mark 11.13), but they have turned red and ripe by May-June. Others do not ripen till autumn: W.R. Telford, *The Barren Temple and the Withered Tree* (Sheffield, 1980), pp. 2f.

25.  Dalman, IV, p. 293.

26.  Dalman, VII, p. 253.

27.  Dalman, IV, p. 297; cf. pp. 314, 318.

28.  See my *The Psalms of the Sons of Korah* (Sheffield, 1982), ch. 5. The site of the courtyard between the city gates at Dan, where the royal wedding took place, has been excavated by Professor A. Biran.

29.  For then the women are merely bidden to see Solomon sitting in his sedan wearing his mother's crown; and there is no event. Also 3.6, 'Who is this . . . ?', must apply to the person, and 'this' is feminine!

30.  See art. 'Dan' in M. Avi-Yonah (ed.), *Encyclopaedia of Archaeological Excavations in the Holy Land* (Oxford, 1975), I, pp. 312ff.

31.  Cf. note 28.

32.  *JBL* 55 (1936), p. 111.

33.  Sheepshearing was a festival in old Israel (Gen. 38.13; 1 Sam. 25; 2 Sam. 13.23ff.), and was probably the pastoral equivalent of the wheat-harvest (Pentecost). Judah offers Tamar a kid for her services as Samson does at the wheat-harvest to his wife (Jg. 15.1).

34.  A less likely derivation would be from the two words *tal*, a heap, *piyyot*, openings, i.e. crenellations.

35.  Cf. W.B. Dinsmoor, *The Architecture of Ancient Greece* (3rd edn; London, 1950), pp. 59ff.

36. It is not likely that pomegranates have any reference to the multiplicity of seeds, i.e. fruitfulness. The Song is nowhere concerned with children, and the Israelites thought of the seeds as all in the father.

37. J.A. St John, *The Hellenes* (London, 1844), writes, 'In the harems of the East the whip is of great service in maintaining order . . . regular floggers, as at our own great schools, always attended'. A classical education is famous for broadening the mind.

38. 'Shir Hashirim Asher Lishelomo', in *Halashon Vehasefer* 2 (Jerusalem, 1951), cited by Gordis; not available to me.

39. W. Rudolph, *Das Buch Ruth. Das Hohelied. Die Klagelieder* (KAT, 17; Gütersloh, 1962), *ad loc.* It is conceivable that we have a hint of the symbols on the tribal standards in the early poem, Jacob's Blessing, in Gen. 49, so that Judah's symbol was the lion, Dan's the serpent, Naphtali's the hind, etc.; and that the same symbols were applied to the constellations, cf. Gen. 37.9. There is, however, no clear evidence of the signs of the Zodiac in Israel until the Christian era.

40. R. de Vaux, *Ancient Israel* (ET; 2nd edn; London, 1965), gives examples of a single queen consort in Egypt, Assyria and among the Hittites, alongside a harem in each case (p. 115).

41. Robert, *ad loc.*

42. But note that the *n* and *m* have been reversed.

43. Cf. Henri Fauconnier, *The Soul of Malaya* (ET; Kuala Lumpur, 1965), p. 44, 'I picked a hibiscus flower and put it in her dark and lustrous hair, which shone with the purple lights that are only seen reflected on women's hair in church'. I am grateful to Michael Counsell for the reference.

44. See BHS.

45. Gordis cites Tur-Sinai again, who offers an Akkadian etymology, *musharu* = membrum virile. See also E. Ben Jehudah, *Thesaurus Totius Hebraitatis* (Jerusalem 1918–), VI, 2980f.

46. I fear to scandalize my readers, especially any who may be religious, or otherwise unmarried, by the variety of sexual practice which seems to be to be implied in the text. I would ask my reader to reflect that sexual manners are as much a matter of social norms as other things; that we have no evidence of puritanism in this area among the Jews; and that we have instances of very religious men in the Christian tradition, like John Donne, who took a great and uninhibited delight in sex. The permissive 1970s are unlikely to have been the first decade in which such freedom was widely practised; and this has seen the publication of books like David Devlin's *The Book of Love* (London, 1974), in which wide sexual variety is commended (and illustrated), with the blessing of the counselling movement. Such activities are not indecent: it is ironic that the Song should have been especially the meditation of monks and nuns over the centuries, when they are the last people for whom it was written.

47. E.g. by Gerleman, with his emphasis on the Egyptian links of the

poem. Lys and others see parts of it, especially the Procession Song, as ancient.

48.  For a review of opinion see J.A. Emerton, 'Wisdom', in G.W. Anderson (ed.), *Tradition and Interpretation* (Oxford, 1979).

49.  J. Winandy, *Le Cantique des Cantiques* (Tournai, 1960), p. 94.

50.  Others suggested as of Persian origin are the words for nard, saffron and nut (Lys, p. 12), and purple (Gordis).

51.  The tract is usually dated within a century of the turn of the era, either way; see M. Philonenko, *Joseph et Aséneth* (Leiden, 1968).

52.  'If you are ashamed of the Song of Songs, hypocrite, you are also ashamed of the woman who conceived you, of the child your wife bore you, most of all, however, of your very self' (J.G. Herder, *Sämmtliche Werke zur Religion und Theologie*, VII [1807], p. 96, cited by Healey, p. 120).

53.  London, 1978, ch. 7.

54.  G. Kisch, *Pseudo-Philo's Liber Antiquitatum Biblicarum* (Notre Dame, Indiana, 1949), 8.8.

55.  *The Evangelists' Calendar*, pp. 19-66.

56.  *The Evangelists' Calendar*, ch. 6, pp. 105-38.

# BIBLIOGRAPHY

Ben-Jehudah, E., *Thesaurus Totius Hebraitatis* (Jerusalem, 1918)
Biran, A., 'Dan', in M.Avi-Yonah (ed.), *Encyclopaedia of Archaeological Excavations in the Holy Land* (Oxford, 1975), I, pp. 312ff.
Dalman, G., *Arbeit und Sitte in Palästina* I-VII (Gütersloh, 1928-1939)
Delitzsch, F., *Hoheslied und Koheleth* (Leipzig, 1875)
Devlin, D., *The Book of Love* (London, 1974)
Dinsmoor, W.B., *The Architecture of Ancient Greece* (3rd edn, London, 1950)
Doughty, C.M., *Travels in Arabia Deserta* (London, 1926)
Emerton, J.A., 'Wisdom', in G.W. Anderson (ed.), *Tradition and Interpretation* (Oxford, 1979)
Exum, J.C., 'A literary and structural analysis of the Song of Songs', *ZAW* (1973), pp. 47-79
Driver, G.R., 'On Supposed Aramaisms in the Old Testament', *JBL* 55 (1936), pp. 101-20
Fauconnierx, H., *The Soul of Malaya* (ET: Kuala Lumpur, 1965)
Gerlemann, G., *Ruth. Das Hohelied* (BKAT 18; Neukirchen-Vluyn, 1965)
Gordis, R., *The Song of Songs and Lamentations* (2nd edn, New York, 1974)
Goulder, M.D., *The Evangelists' Calendar* (London, 1978)
Goulder, M.D., *The Psalms of the Sons of Korah* (Sheffield, 1982)
Healey, J.F., 'The Song of Songs', in J.H. Eaton (ed.), *Readings in Biblical Hebrew II* (Birmingham, 1972)
Herder, J.G., *Sämmtliche Werke zur Religion und Theologie* I-XII (Tübingen, 1805-1820)
Jastrow, M. *A Dictionary of the Targumim, the Talmud Babli and Yerushalmi, and the Midrashic Literature* (New York, 1975)
Kisch, G., *Pseudo-Philo's Liber Antiquitatum Biblicarum* (Notre Dame, Indiana, 1949)
Landy, F., *Paradoxes of Paradise* (Sheffield, 1983)
Löw, I., *Die Flora der Juden, I-III* (Vienna, Leipzig, 1924-8)
Lys, D., *'Le Plus Beau Chant' de la Création* (LD 51; Paris, 1968)
May, H.G. (ed.), *Oxford Bible Atlas* (2nd edn; Oxford, 1974)
Meek, T.J., 'Introduction and Interpretation of the Song of Songs', in *The Interpreter's Bible* (New York/Nashville, 1956) V, pp. 98-148
Ouweneel, W.J., *Das Lied der Lieder* (Wuppertal, 1976)
Philonenko, M., *Joseph et Aséneth* (Leiden, 1968)
Pope, M.H., *Song of Songs* (AB; New York, 1977)
Robert, A., *Le Cantique des Cantiques* (completed by R. Tournay, with A. Feuillet; Paris, 1963)
Rowley, H.H., *The Servant of the Lord, and Other Essays in the Old Testament* (London, 1952)
Rudolph, W., *Das Buch Ruth. Das Hohelied. Die Klagelieder* (KAT 17; Gütersloh, 1962)
St John, J.A., *The Hellenes* (London, 1844)
Telford, W.R., *The Barren Temple and the Withered Tree* (Sheffield, 1980)

Tur-Sinai, N.H., 'Shir Hashirim Asher Lishelomo', *Halashon Vehasefer* 2 (Jerusalem, 1951)

de Vaux, R., *Ancient Israel* (ET, 2nd ed.; London, 1965)

Winandy, J., *Le Cantique des Cantiques* (Tournai, 1960)

Zohary, M., *Plants of the Bible* (Cambridge, 1982)

# INDEX OF BIBLICAL AND RABBINIC PASSAGES

*Genesis*
| | |
|---|---|
| 18 | 6 |
| 24 | 13 |
| 25.2 | 12 |
| 27.37 | 20 |
| 29.27 | 11 |
| 30.13 | 51, 82 |
| 30.14f. | 61 |
| 30.38, 41 | 57, 83 |
| 31.23 | 33 |
| 32.2 | 55, 83 |
| 36.33f. | 81 |
| 37 | 49, 81, 83 |
| 37.9 | 83, 89 |
| 37.16 | 13, 83 |
| 37.25 | 83 |
| 38 | 81 |
| 38.12 | 83 |
| 38.13 | 88 |
| 38.14 | 13 |
| 38.17 | 83 |
| 38.18 | 65, 83 |
| 38.27 | 83 |
| 40.10 | 84 |
| 41 | 81 |
| 41.42 | 65, 84 |
| 49 | 89 |

*Exodus*
| | |
|---|---|
| 2.16 | 57 |
| 25.9 | 50 |

*Numbers*
| | |
|---|---|
| 1–4 | 50 |

*Deuteronomy*
| | |
|---|---|
| 20.10 | 66 |
| 22.13ff | 27, 39 |

*Judges*
| | |
|---|---|
| 5.7 | 74 |
| 5.20 | 51 |
| 9.46ff | 33 |
| 15.1 | 88 |
| 16.13 | 57 |

| | |
|---|---|
| 16.29 | 20 |

*Ruth*
| | |
|---|---|
| 1–4 | 75f, 81 |
| 3.6-9 | 25 |

*1 Samuel*
| | |
|---|---|
| 1–4 | 81 |
| 9.27 | 23 |
| 16.12 | 45 |
| 25 | 88 |

*2 Samuel*
| | |
|---|---|
| 2.28 | 23 |
| 6.16 | 51 |
| 13.23f | 83 |
| 14.2 | 13 |
| 19.35 | 73 |

*1 Kings*
| | |
|---|---|
| 1.38 | 29 |
| 1.44 | 29 |
| 2.17ff | 55 |
| 2.19 | 30 |
| 4.32 | 73 |
| 6.34 | 18, 45 |
| 7.2ff | 18 |
| 8.27 | 11 |
| 10 | 85 |
| 10.13 | 88 |
| 11.3 | 50 |
| 13.4 | 41 |
| 22.39 | 56 |

*2 Kings*
| | |
|---|---|
| 4.39 | 33 |
| 10.3 | 12 |
| 10.28f | 17 |

*1 Chronicles*
| | |
|---|---|
| 5.19 | 52 |
| 5.23 | 37 |

*2 Chronicles*
| | |
|---|---|
| 3.14 | 12 |

*Nehemiah*
| | |
|---|---|
| 2.8 | 73 |
| 3.15 | 38 |

*Esther*
| | |
|---|---|
| 1.12 | 33 |
| 1.16 | 46 |

*Job*
| | |
|---|---|
| 1f, 42 | 9, 81 |
| 1.15 | 12 |
| 7.4 | 25 |

*Psalms*
| | |
|---|---|
| 1 | 85 |
| 7.15 | 65 |
| 19.4ff | 86 |
| 20.7 | 49 |
| 42.4 | 42 |
| 45.8 | 29, 39, 56 |
| 45.15 | 12 |
| 68.14 | 11 |
| 91.5 | 29 |
| 92.11 | 11 |
| 119.103 | 86 |
| 119.147 | 25 |
| 121.6 | 29 |
| 133.2 | 45 |

*Proverbs*
| | |
|---|---|
| 1.1 | 72 |
| 3.3 | 65 |
| 3.8 | 56 |
| 7.13 | 62 |
| 8.19 | 85 |
| 23.31 | 58, 73 |
| 25.12 | 55 |

*Ecclesiastes*
| | |
|---|---|
| 1.1 | 72 |
| 2.5 | 73 |
| 7.1 | 11 |

*Isaiah*
| | |
|---|---|
| 3.23 | 42 |

| Isaiah (cont.) | | 13 | 81 | Targ. Y. Lev. | |
|---|---|---|---|---|---|
| 5.1 | 69, 85 | 13.7 | 37, 84 | 6.5 | 33 |
| 7.23 | 69, 85 | 13.15 | 85 | | |
| 13 | 81, 85 | 14.4-7 | 84 | m. Sabb. | |
| 13.20 | 13, 85 | | | 6.3 | 17 |
| 26.7 | 58 | Joel | | | |
| 38.12 | 57 | 1.12 | 19, 85 | b. Sabb. | |
| 54.6 | 49 | | | 63a | 17 |
| 56.5 | 9 | Amos | | | |
| 61.10 | 30 | 3.15 | 56 | t. Sanh. | |
| | | | | 12.10 | 73, 86 |
| Jeremiah | | Tobit | | | |
| 32.10 | 65 | 7.12, 16 | 37 | m. Yad. | |
| | | | | 3.5 | 73 |
| Ezekiel | | 1 Maccabees | | | |
| 1.16 | 45 | 4.57 | 34 | Gen. R. | |
| 16.4 | 56 | | | 95 | 5, 45 |
| 16 | 49 | Mark | | | |
| 23 | 49 | 11.13 | 88 | Cant. R. | |
| 27.11 | 33 | | | 5.14 | 6 |
| 31.5 | 38 | Revelation | | | |
| | | 21.2 | 49f | Yalkut Cant. | |
| Hosea | | | | 991 | 6 |
| 3.1 | 20 | Joseph and | | | |
| 11.4 | 11 | Aseneth | 76 | | |

# JOURNAL FOR THE STUDY OF THE OLD TESTAMENT
Supplement Series

1  I, HE, WE AND THEY:
   A LITERARY APPROACH TO ISAIAH 53
   D.J.A. Clines

4  THANKSGIVING FOR A LIBERATED PROPHET:
   AN INTERPRETATION OF ISAIAH CHAPTER 53
   R.N. Whybray

5  REDATING THE EXODUS AND CONQUEST
   J.J. Bimson

6  THE STORY OF KING DAVID:
   GENRE AND INTERPRETATION
   D.M. Gunn

7  THE SENSE OF BIBLICAL NARRATIVE I:
   STRUCTURAL ANALYSES IN THE HEBREW BIBLE (2nd edition)
   D. Jobling

10 THE THEME OF THE PENTATEUCH
   D.J.A. Clines

12 THE JUST KING:
   MONARCHICAL JUDICIAL AUTHORITY IN ANCIENT ISRAEL
   K.W. Whitelam

13 ISAIAH AND THE DELIVERANCE OF JERUSALEM:
   R.E. Clements

14 THE FATE OF KING SAUL:
   AN INTERPRETATION OF A BIBLICAL STORY
   D.M. Gunn

15 THE DEUTERONOMISTIC HISTORY
   M. Noth

16 PROPHECY AND ETHICS:
   ISAIAH AND THE ETHICAL TRADITIONS OF ISRAEL
   E.W. Davies

17 THE ROLES OF ISRAEL'S PROPHETS
   D.L. Petersen

18 THE DOUBLE REDACTION OF THE DEUTERONOMISTIC HISTORY
   R.D.Nelson

19 ART AND MEANING:
   RHETORIC IN BIBLICAL LITERATURE
   Edited by D.J.A. Clines, D.M. Gunn, & A.J. Hauser

20 THE PSALMS OF THE SONS OF KORAH
   M.D. Goulder

21 COLOUR TERMS IN THE OLD TESTAMENT
   A. Brenner

22 AT THE MOUNTAIN OF GOD:
   STORY AND THEOLOGY IN EXODUS 32–34
   R.W.L. Moberly

23 THE GLORY OF ISRAEL:
   THE THEOLOGY AND PROVENIENCE OF THE ISAIAH TARGUM
   B.D. Chilton

24 MIDIAN, MOAB AND EDOM:
 THE HISTORY AND ARCHAEOLOGY OF LATE BRONZE AND IRON AGE
 JORDAN AND NORTH-WEST ARABIA
 Edited by J.F.A. Sawyer & D.J.A Clines

25 THE DAMASCUS COVENANT:
 AN INTERPRETATION OF THE 'DAMASCUS DOCUMENT'
 P.R. Davies

26 CLASSICAL HEBREW POETRY:
 A GUIDE TO ITS TECHNIQUES
 W.G.E. Watson

27 PSALMODY AND PROPHECY
 W.H. Bellinger

28 HOSEA: AN ISRAELITE PROPHET IN JUDEAN PERSPECTIVE
 G.I. Emmerson

29 EXEGESIS AT QUMRAN:
 4QFLORILEGIUM IN ITS JEWISH CONTEXT
 G.J. Brooke

30 THE ESTHER SCROLL:
 THE STORY OF THE STORY
 D.J.A. Clines

31 IN THE SHELTER OF ELYON:
 ESSAYS IN HONOR OF G.W. AHLSTRÖM
 Edited by W.B. Barrick & J.R. Spencer

32 THE PROPHETIC PERSONA:
 JEREMIAH AND THE LANGUAGE OF THE SELF
 T. Polk

33 LAW AND THEOLOGY IN DEUTERONOMY
 J.G. McConville

34 THE TEMPLE SCROLL:
 AN INTRODUCTION, TRANSLATION AND COMMENTARY
 J. Maier

35 SAGA, LEGEND, TALE, NOVELLA, FABLE:
 NARRATIVE FORMS IN OLD TESTAMENT LITERATURE
 Edited by G.W. Coats

36 THE SONG OF FOURTEEN SONGS
 M.D. Goulder

37 UNDERSTANDING THE WORD:
 ESSAYS IN HONOR OF BERNHARD W. ANDERSON
 Edited by J.T. Butler, E.W. Conrad & B.C. Ollenburger

42 A WORD IN SEASON:
 ESSAYS IN HONOUR OF WILLIAM McKANE
 Edited by J.D. Martin & P.R. Davies

43 THE CULT OF MOLEK:
 A REASSESSMENT
 G.C. Heider

47 THE GREEK TEXT OF JEREMIAH:
 A REVISED HYPOTHESIS
 S. Soderlund